Rumi

Jeremy P. Tarcher/
Putnam

a member of
Penguin Putnam Inc.
New York

Rumi

In the Arms of the Beloved

TRANSLATIONS BY

JONATHAN STAR

I would like to thank all those people who have supported this offering with their love and enthusiasm. Special thanks go to Shahram Shiva for supplying literal translations of the quatrains, and to all the people at Jeremy P. Tarcher for the care and honor that they extended to these words.

Most Tarcher/Putnam books are available at special quantity discounts for bulk purchases for sales promotions, premiums, fund-raising, and educational needs. Special books or book excerpts also can be created to fit specific needs. For details, write or telephone Putnam Special Markets, 200 Madison Avenue, New York, NY 10016; (212) 951-8891.

Jeremy P. Tarcher/Putnam
a member of
Penguin Putnam Inc.
200 Madison Avenue
New York, NY 10016
http://www.putnam.com

Library of Congress Cataloging-in-Publication Data

Jalāl ad-Dīn Rūmī, Maulana, 1207–1273.
[Selections. English. 1997]
Rumi : in the arms of the beloved / translations by Jonathan Star.
p.   cm.
ISBN 0-87477-894-8
1. Sufi poetry, Persian—Translations into English.   I. Star, Jonathan.
PK6480.E5S737   1997   97-13844 CIP
891'.5511—dc21

Printed in the United States of America
2   4   6   8   10   9   7   5   3   1

This book is printed on acid-free paper. ∞

Book design by Deborah Kerner

To one
who wears
the robes of fire

Contents

Introduction ◆ xi

Part One. To Us Return ◆ 1

Part Two. The Beloved ◆ 23

Part Three. An Endless Celebration ◆ 51

Part Four. The Cauldron of Love ◆ 87

Part Five. A Mine of Rubies ◆ 117

Part Six. The Bliss of Union ◆ 165

Part Seven. Stories ◆ 187

Terms and Symbolism ◆ 195

Sources ◆ 203

Index ◆ 205

Introduction

There is a voice in us all that is ever-present, a voice that always sings its melody to the world. This is the voice of truth and certainty, the voice that lays bare the hidden mysteries of the soul. In a burst of inspiration, the German poet Rainer Maria Rilke heard this voice and wrote for three days "in a single breathless obedience . . . without one word being in doubt or having to be changed."

This inspired state that opens up the vistas of the universe—one we glimpse only at peak moments in our life—is the same state that poet-saints live in all the time. That is why their every word is charged with purity and divine refulgence; their poetry is a reflection of their own perfect state. Jalaluddin Rumi was such a poet-saint. For thirty years poetry issued from his lips, infused with such genius and perfection as to belie human origin. He was a pure instrument of the Divine, a flute upon which God played an exquisite song. In one of his quatrains, Rumi writes:

Do you think I know what I'm doing,
That for a moment, or even half a moment,
   I know what verses will come from my mouth?

I am no more than a pen in a writer's hand,
No more than a ball smacked around by a polo stick!

Rumi's "breathless obedience" to that inner voice is what made him a peerless master of ecstatic verse. The Islamic scholar A. J. Arberry writes, "In Rumi we encounter one of the world's greatest poets. In profundity of thought, inventiveness of image, and triumphant mastery of language, he stands out as the supreme genius of Islamic mysticism." And R. A. Nicholson, who dedicated his life to Islamic studies, called Rumi "the greatest mystical poet of any age."

The poetic and mystical achievement of Jalaluddin Rumi is a monument in the annals of spiritual literature. In his vast outpouring he not only captured the whole of Islamic mysticism but polished it, refined it, and transformed it into a thing of exquisite beauty. The most personal experiences are cast in the light of universal truths; the ordinary life of man—crowded, busy, and full of uncertainty—is shown to be a necessary step on one's journey to the ineffable Absolute. Rumi has given every word life; and everyone who reads him beholds the naked words of the soul clothed in living form. In Rumi we hear the pure voice of love—we hear the intimate whispers of lover and beloved, we feel the joyous heart gliding upon the water of its own melting.

Symbols of Grace

Sufi poetry is filled with metaphors, the most striking of which revolve around wine, taverns, and drunkenness. In this symbolic language of love, "wine" represents the divine love that intoxicates the soul; "getting drunk" means losing oneself in that love; the "cup" refers to one's body and mind; and the *Saaqi* (the Cupbearer, the Maiden who pours the wine) is the grace-bestowing aspect of God that fills the soul's empty cup with the wine of love. The Sufis even have a word for "hangover" which suggests the lingering effects of love.

These metaphors of drunkenness are, more than anything else, a call to experience; they reflect the Sufi sentiment that the immediate experience of God is far more crucial than any kind of objective or learned knowledge. In a verse from his famous *Rubá'iyát,* Omar Khayyám writes:

> The cover on the wine-vat is happier
> > than the empire of King Jamshid,
> The wine more fragrant than a great feast,
> The first sigh of a drunk lover's heart
> > more blessed than the song of the greatest poet.

Although Rumi employed the macabre and bacchanalian symbolism of his tradition, his more endearing themes were based on symbols related to nature. In his poetic verse, the *nightingale* represents the soul; the *rose* is the perfect beauty of God; the *rosegarden* is paradise; and the *breeze* is God's life-giving breath. When we hear of *Winter,* it is a soul separated from God; when we hear of *Spring,* it is union, resurrection, and rebirth. All the elements of nature that come alive in Spring are the outward signs of the soul's inner awakening: the rising Sun is the illumination of divine knowledge, the "festival of color" is the beauty of the soul's awakening, and the warm rain is the pouring down of God's grace.

❖

The Sun had a special significance for Rumi because it alluded to his master, Shams—the one who awakened the truth within Rumi. Rumi's use of the terms "Shams," "Shams-e Tabriz" (Shams of Tabriz), and "Shamsuddin" refers not only to his master but also to the many aspects of the Beloved, embodied in Shams: "Shams" symbolizes the power of grace, the power that awakens the truth within us; "Shams" symbolizes the inner sunrise, the inner light of consciousness, one's own soul and its awakening. Rumi writes:

> O my soul, where can I find rest
>   but in the shimmering love of his heart?
> Where can I see the pure light of the Sun
>   but in the eyes of my own Shams-e Tabriz?

The Meeting of Two Oceans

By all accounts, Rumi lived a grand and illustrious life—he was a respected teacher, a master of Sufi lore, the head of a university in the Anatolian capital city of Konya (in present-day Turkey). At the age of thirty-four he claimed hundreds of disciples, the king being one of them. And what is so remarkable and unforgettable about Rumi's life is that in one moment all this changed—the moment he met a wandering darvish named Shams-e Tabriz.

There are several accounts of this historic meeting. One version says that during a lecture of Rumi's, Shams came in and dumped all of Rumi's books—one handwritten by his own father—into a pool of water. Rumi thought the books were destroyed, but Shams retrieved them, volume by volume, intact. Another version says that at a wave of Shams' hand, Rumi's books were engulfed in flames and burned to ashes. Shams then put his hand in the ashes and pulled out

the books. (A story much like the first.) A third account says that Rumi was riding on a mule through a square in the center of Konya. A crowd of eager students walked by his feet. Suddenly a strange figure dressed in black fur approached Rumi, grabbed hold of his mule's bridle, and said: "O scholar of infinite knowledge, who was greater, Muhammad or Bayazid of Bestam?" This seemed like an absurd question since, in all of Islam, Muhammad was held supreme among all the prophets. Rumi replied, "How can you ask such a question?—No one can compare with Muhammad."
"O then," Shams asked, "why did Muhammad say, 'We have not known Thee, O God, as thou should be known,' whereas Bayazid said, 'Glory unto me! I know the full glory of God'?"

With this one simple question—and with the piercing gaze of Shams' eyes—Rumi's entire view of reality changed. The question was merely an excuse. Shams' imparting of an inner awakening is what shattered Rumi's world. The truths and assumptions upon which Rumi based his whole life crumbled. This same story is told symbolically in the first two accounts, whereby Rumi's books—representing all his acquired intellectual knowledge, including the knowledge given to him by his father—are destroyed, and then miraculously retrieved or "resurrected" by Shams. The books coming from the ashes, created anew by Shams, represent the replacing of Rumi's book-learned knowledge (and his lofty regard for such knowledge) with divine knowledge and the direct experience of God.

According to an embellished version of this third account, after Shams' question, Rumi entered a mystical state of ego annihilation that the Sufis call *fana*. When he regained consciousness, he looked at Shams with utter amazement, realizing that this was no ordinary darvish, but the Beloved himself in human form. From that moment on, Rumi's life was never again the same. He took Shams to live in his home and the two men were inseparable; they spent hours a day together, sometimes isolating themselves for long periods to pray and fast in divine communion with God.

About this meeting, Rumi's son Sultan Walad wrote: "After meeting Shams, my father danced all day and sang all night. He had been a scholar—he became a poet. He had been an ascetic—he became drunk with love."

Rumi was totally lost in this newfound love that his master revealed, and all his great attainments were blossoming through that love. Every day was a miracle, a new birth for Rumi's soul. He had found the Beloved, he had finally been shown the glory of his own soul.

Then, suddenly, eighteen months after Shams entered Rumi's life, he was gone. He returned some time later, for a brief period, and then he was gone again forever. Some accounts say that Shams left in the middle of the night and that Rumi wandered in search of him for two years. (Perhaps a symbolic and romantic portrayal of the lover in search of his missing Beloved.) Other accounts report that Shams was murdered by Rumi's jealous disciples (symbolizing how one's desires and lower tendencies can destroy the thing held most dear).

Without Shams, Rumi found himself in a state of utter and incurable despair; and his whole life thereafter became one of longing and divine remembrance. Rumi's emptiness was that of a person who has just lost a husband or a wife, or a dear friend. Rumi's story shows us that the longing and emptiness we feel for a lost loved one is only a reflection, a hologram, of the

longing we feel for God; it is the longing we feel to become whole again, the longing to return to the root
from which we were cut. (Rumi uses the metaphor of a
reed cut from a reed bed and then made into a flute—
which becomes a symbol of a human separated from its
source, the Beloved. And as the reed flute wails all day,
telling about its separation from the reed bed, so Rumi
wails all day telling about being separated from his
Beloved.)

It was Shams' disappearance, however, that ig-
nited the fire of longing within Rumi; and it was this
very longing that brought him the glorious union with
the Beloved. Years later Rumi wrote: "It is the burn of
the heart that I want. It is this burning which is everything—more precious than a worldly empire—because
it calls God secretly in the night."

The Path of Love

In Rumi's poetry, love is the soul of the universe,
and this soul knows no bounds—it embraces all people,
all countries, and all religions. The goal of Sufism is
to know love in all of its glorious forms; and every
prophet, every practice, and every form of worship that
leads toward love is, in essence, Sufism. The great Sufi
philosopher Ibn Arabi writes:

> My heart holds within it every form,
>   it contains a pasture for gazelles,
>   a monastery for Christian monks.
> There is a temple for idol-worshippers,
>   a holy shrine for pilgrims;
> There is the table of the Torah,
>   and the Book of the Koran.

I follow the religion of Love
and go whichever way His camel leads me.
This is the true faith;
This is the true religion.

    Just as the Sufis honored all traditions, seeing
each as a path leading to the highest truth, they also
honored the prophets of these traditions. They looked
upon each for guidance and inspiration. Many Sufis,
including the great Mansur al-Hallaj, idealized Jesus as
the embodiment of perfect love; they built their philos-
ophy around him, rather than the Prophet. The
renowned Sufi saint Junayd gives this prescription for
Sufi practice based on the lives of the prophets:

> *Sufism is founded on the eight qualities exemplified
> by the eight prophets: The generosity of Abraham,
> who was willing to sacrifice his son. The surrender of
> Ishmael, who submitted to the command of God and
> gave up his dear life. The patience of Job, who en-
> dured the affliction of worms and the jealousy of the
> Merciful. The mystery of Zacharias, to whom God
> said, "Thou shalt not speak unto men for three days
> save by sign." The solitude of John, who was a
> stranger in his own country and an alien to his own
> kind. The detachment of Jesus, who was so removed
> from worldly things that he kept only a cup and a
> comb—the cup he threw away when he saw a man
> drinking in the palms of his hand, and the comb
> likewise when he saw another man using his fingers
> instead of a comb. The wearing of wool by Moses,
> whose garment was woolen. And the poverty of
> Muhammad, to whom God sent the key of all trea-
> sures that are upon the face of the earth.*

The supreme vision of Sufism is to see God everywhere, to view every part of creation as a reflection of God's glory. The poet Jami writes: "Every branch and leaf and fruit reveals some aspect of God's perfection: the cypress gives hint of His majesty; the rose gives tidings of His beauty." Every atom was created by God so that man could know the highest truth and learn the secrets of love.

◈

Rumi's poetry has the magical ability to show us this truth and to unlock love's precious secrets. Within the folds of his words we gain entrance to a hidden chamber; we hear whispers that are ancient, yet intimate; we behold the endless love story between the individual soul and God. Like looking into a polished mirror, or like being in the presence of a holy being, reading Rumi's poetry shows us ourselves and our state, but more than that, it shows us the boundless glory of what we can become.

Day and night my father danced in ecstasy,
Spinning on earth like the turning heavens.
His laughter echoed through the zenith of the sky
And was heard by beings of every realm.
He showered the musicians with gold and silver.
He gave away whatever came into his hand.
He was never without a singing heart.
He was never at rest.

There was a rebellion in the city—
No, the whole world sounded with the cries of rebellion.
How could a great pillar and champion of Islam,
Hailed as the leader of both worlds,
Become such a raving madman?

Those who recited the scriptures
Were now singing with abandon
And swaying with the musicians.
In public and in private
People turned away from dogma and empty rituals
And went crazy after love!

—Sultan Walad
(Rumi's son)

Rumi

Part One

To

Us

Return

We Can See the Truth in Your Eyes

For ages you have come and gone
    courting this delusion.
For ages you have run from the pain
    and forfeited the ecstasy.
So come, return to the root of the root
    of your own soul.

Although you appear in earthly form
Your essence is pure Consciousness.
You are the fearless guardian
    of Divine Light.
So come, return to the root of the root
    of your own soul.

When you lose all sense of self
    the bonds of a thousand chains will vanish.
Lose yourself completely,
Return to the root of the root
    of your own soul.

You descended from Adam, by the pure Word of God,
    but you turned your sight
    to the empty show of this world.
Alas, how can you be satisfied with so little?
So come, return to the root of the root
    of your own soul.

Why are you so enchanted by this world
    when a mine of gold lies within you?

Open your eyes and come—
Return to the root of the root
    of your own soul.

You were born from the rays of God's Majesty
    when the stars were in their perfect place.
How long will you suffer from the blows
    of a nonexistent hand?
So come, return to the root of the root
    of your own soul.

You are a ruby encased in granite.
How long will you deceive Us with this outer show?
O friend, We can see the truth in your eyes!
So come, return to the root of the root
    of your own soul.

After one moment with that glorious Friend
    you became loving, radiant, and ecstatic.
Your eyes were sweet and full of fire.
Come, return to the root of the root
    of your own soul.

Shams-e Tabriz, the King of the Tavern,
    has handed you an eternal cup,
And God in all His glory is pouring the wine.
So come! Drink!
Return to the root of the root
    of your own soul.

Soul of all souls, life of all life—you are That.
Seen and unseen, moving and unmoving—you are That.
The road that leads to the City is endless;
Go without head or feet
    and you'll already be there.
What else could you be?—you are That.

Don't Go Without Me

Dancing in ecstasy you go,
    my soul of souls—
Don't go without me.
Laughing with your friends
    you enter the garden—
Don't go without me.

    Don't let the sky turn without me.
    Don't let the Moon shine without me.
    Don't let the Earth spin without me.
    Don't let the days pass without me.

The two worlds are joyous
    because of you.
Don't stay in this world without me.
Don't go to the next world without me.

    Don't let your eyes look without me.
    Don't let your tongue speak without me.
    Don't let your hands hold without me.
    Don't let your soul stir without me.

Moonlight reveals the sky's bright face.
I am the light, you are the Moon—
Don't rise without me.

The thorn is protected by the rose!
You are the rose, I am the thorn—
Don't show your beauty without me.

I am the curve of your mallet,
    the bits of stone beneath your chisel.
Don't strike the stone without me,
Don't move the chisel without me.

O joyous companion of the King,
Don't drink without me.
O watchman on the rooftop,
Don't stay up without me.

Woe to those who travel alone. . . .
You know every sign,
You've walked upon every path—
    Don't go without me.

Some call you love,
I call you the *King of Love.*
You are beyond all imaginings,
    taking me places
        I can't even dream of.
O Ruler of my Heart,
    wherever you go . . .

        Don't go without me.

In the heavens I see your eyes,
In your eyes I see the heavens.

Why look for another Moon
    or another Sun?—
What I see will always be enough for me.

By the Curl of My Hair

The King held counsel with a group of madmen.
All at once their tormented souls began to cry out.

My voice was free of its beastly nature
And the King heard it above the rest.
He signaled the guards
    to put that madman back in chains.

"O King, if I am mad,
    you are the Solomon of every mad spirit.
O King, you know the language of the birds
    and the spell of magicians.
Why use chains on me?
Can't you cast a spell on this madman?"

An old man approached the King and said,
    "Bind him in chains.
    This madman will spread havoc
    through both worlds."

The King said,
"This madman cannot be held by chains,
    only by the curl of my hair.
You do not know him as I do.
He will break a hundred fetters
    if they keep him from my hand.

"This one knows but three words,
'To Us Return,'
For he is the King's falcon."

A Thousand Souls of Mine

◆

Lord of Beauty, Lord of Grace,
Enter my soul
   like one who enters a garden in bloom.

One glance from you and stones turn to rubies.
One hint from you
   and every goal is within reach.

Come, come, you are the life and salvation of man.
Come, come, you are the eye and light of Joseph.
Touch my head
   for your touch removes
   the darkness of the body.

Come, come, for you bestow beauty and grace.
Come, come, for you are the cure of a thousand ills.
Come, come, even though you have never left—
   come and hear some poetry.
Sit in the place of my soul,
   for you are a thousand souls of mine.

Begone with your cares and your ancient longings—
   you are the Beloved!

If the King did not sit
   on the throne of this world
There would be darkness and confusion.

You are joyous and alive by His breath.
You move by the power of His love.
Now, like an artist, you create.
Now, like a servant, you sweep the floor.

Everything you touch
    will reach its goal
    and fly with the wings of an angel. . . .
But wings cannot carry you to God.
Like the mule that carried the Prophet,
Only love can carry you there.

The Return

My soul wants to fly away
When your Presence calls it so sweetly.
My soul wants to take flight
When you whisper, "Arise."

A fish wants to dive from dry land
    into the ocean
      when it hears the roaring waves.
A falcon wants to return from the forest
    to the King's wrist
      when it hears the drum beating "Return."
A Sufi, shimmering with light,
    wants to dance like a sunbeam
      when darkness surrounds him.

O God—you are the graceful and the beautiful,
    you are the highest love,
    you are the giver of life.
What misery and hardship comes
    to those who turn away from you!

O bird, fly back to your native land.
You have broken free from your cage;
Your wings are eager for flight.

Fly from the brackish puddle
    toward the flowing waters of life!
Leave the room where they put the dirty sandals
    and return to the royal seat of the soul!

Be off! Be off!
O soul, leave behind this world of separation
    and come with us to the world of union.
How long will you play in this dusty world
    like a child filling his skirt with worthless stones?

Cast away the burdens of the earth
    and fly upward toward heaven!
Put away your childish care
    and join the royal banquet.

Behold the countless ways this body has entrapped you!
Break its deadly hold.
Rise up, lift your head clear of this delusion.

Reach for the Holy Book with your right hand
You are not like a child
    who doesn't know right from left.

God said to the mind, "Return from where you came."
He said to the hand of Death,
    "Grab hold of worldly men."
He said to the soul, "Fly to the Unseen.
    Take all the treasure you can carry
    and cry no more."

You ask, "Who is the King?"—
Tell the world that you are the King!

Your knowledge has brought the question,
And your grace has given the answer.

Song to My Soul

Remember what I said. . . .
I said, *Don't leave, for I am your Friend.*
In the mirage of this world
    I am the fountain of life.
Even if you leave in anger
    and stay away for a thousand years
You will return to me,
    for I am your goal.

I said, Don't be content with worldly promises
    for I am the tabernacle of your contentment.

I said, Do not go upon the dry land
    for I am the Sea without a shore.

I said, O bird, do not fly into the hunter's net;
Come toward me, for I am the power
    that moves your wings,
    that lifts you through the sky.

I said, They'll capture you and put you on ice;
    I am the fire and the warmth
    of your true yearning.

I said, They will cover you with water and clay;
    You will forget that I am your taintless beginning.

I said, No one can tell how my work will manifest
        for I create the world from all sides.

Let your heart's light guide you to my house.
Let your heart's light show you that we are one.

All My Youth Returns

You are the comfort of my soul
 in the season of sorrow.
You are the wealth of my spirit
 in the heartbreak of loss.

The unimaginable,
The unknowable—
That is what you give my soul
 when it moves in your direction.

By your grace
 my eyes have looked upon eternity.
O King, how could this crumbling empire
 ever take me from you?

The voice that sings your name
 is sweeter than midnight sleep
 more graceful than the song of a royal poet.

When deep in prayer
 my faith is bound by the thought of you,
 not the seven verses of faith.

 You greet sinners with mercy,
 You melt stone hearts with love.

If I were offered a kingdom,
And the world's riches were placed at my feet,
I would bow with my face low and say,
 This does not compare to His love!

Union is the pure wine.
My life is the cup.
Without your wine
    what use is this cup?

I once had a thousand desires,
But in my one desire to know you
    all else melted away.
The pure essence of your being
    has taken over my heart and soul.
Now there is no second or third,
    only the sound of your sweet cry.
Through your grace I have found
    a treasure within myself.
I have found the truth of the Unseen world.
I have come upon the eternal ecstasy.
I have gone beyond the ravages of time.
I have become one with you!
Now my heart sings,
    "I am the soul of the world."

From my first breath I have longed for Him—
This longing has become my life.
This longing has seen me grow old. . . .

But one mention of Shams-e Tabriz
    and all my youth comes back to me.

On the First Day

♦

I was there on the first day,
Before anything had a name.
On that day
    there was neither "I" nor "We."
Every name, and everything named,
    came after me.

Within one curl of the Beloved's hair
I saw the birth of creation.
I saw every name forming,
    every object coming into view.
Yet there was no curl!

♦

I looked upon every Cross, in every church,
    yet He was not there.
I went to the temples of India
    and the shrines of China
    yet He was not there.
I searched the mountains of Herat and Candalar
    yet He was not there.
I scaled the distant peak of Mount Qaf
    only to find
    the empty nest of the Phoenix.
I visited the Ka'be
    but He was not in that tourist site
    amidst pilgrims young and old.

I read the books of Avicenna
    but His wisdom went beyond all the words.
I went to the highest court,
    within the distance of "two bow-lengths,"
    but He was not there.

Then I looked within my own heart
    and there I found Him—
    He was nowhere else.

Last night you fell asleep on me!
And tonight you toss and turn
    only pretending to be asleep.
We will be together until the Day of Resurrection.
So let me hear those words again—
    the ones you told me last night in your sleep!

Song of the Reed*

Listen to the song of the reed,
How it wails with the pain of separation:

"Ever since I was taken from my reed bed
My woeful song has caused men and women to weep.
I seek out those whose hearts are torn by separation
For only they understand the pain of this longing.
Whoever is taken away from his homeland
Yearns for the day he will return.
In every gathering, among those who are happy or sad,
I cry with the same lament.
Everyone hears according to his own understanding,
None has searched for the secrets within me.
My secret is found in my lament—
But an eye or ear without light cannot know it. . . ."

The sound of the reed comes from fire, not wind—
What use is one's life without this fire?
It is the fire of love that brings music to the reed.
It is the ferment of love that gives taste to the wine.
The song of the reed soothes the pain of lost love.
Its melody sweeps the veils from the heart.
Can there be a poison so bitter or a sugar so sweet
As the song of the reed?
To hear the song of the reed
        everything you have ever known must be left behind.

*These lines form the opening of Rumi's most famous work, the Masnavi.

Part Two

The

Beloved

There is a place where words are born of silence,
A place where the whispers of the heart arise.

There is a place where voices sing your beauty,
A place where every breath
   carves your image
   in my soul.

O Beloved,
Be Like That to Me

The flames that dance with love—
O Beloved, be like that to me.
The burning heat within the fire—
O Beloved, be like that to me.

My candle burns with longing.
It cries with tears of wax.
Like the wick of a melting candle—
O Beloved, be like that to me.

Now that we've joined the path of love
    we cannot sleep at night.
At the drunken tavern, the drummer beats the drum—
O Beloved, be like that to me.

The night is dark, the lovers are awake.
Don't bother them with thoughts of sleep.
They want only to be here with us—
O Beloved, be like that to me.

Union is a raging river running toward the sea.
Tonight the moon kisses the stars,
    Majnun becomes Layla—
O Beloved, be like that to me.

God has become everything.
He has graced this poet with kindness.
Everything I touch and see becomes the fire of love—
O Beloved, be like that to me.

The day your love touches me
I'll become so mad that lunatics will run away.

The words of a master-poet could never capture
the spell that your eyelashes cast upon my heart.

He Also Made the Key

When I entered the city
    you moved away.
When I left the city
    you didn't even look up to say good-bye.

I'll accept your kindness,
I'll accept your insult.
I'll accept whatever you have to give.

Your radiance shines
    in every atom of creation
    yet our petty desires keep it hidden.

Like the beautiful wife of a prince
You dwell in a lonely place.
If you came out of hiding
    the veil on every face would fall.

You confound the doubting heart,
You intoxicate the faithful head.
You have robbed every soul of its senses,
You have brought every heart to your breast.

All roses fall prey to December.
All intellect falls prey to love's glory.

Since the rose is not eternal
Why be captured by its scent?
Let me know your secrets—
Only the ones that last forever.

How many men have found tragic ends
    running after beauty?
Why don't they look for you?—
    the heart and spirit of all beauty.

You formed man from a handful of dust.
You gave him the power to know the highest truth.
You freed him from the snares of this world
    with one breath of your spirit.

O love,
O heart,
Find the way to heaven.
Find the way to God's pasture.
You have spent enough time
    in this pasture made for cattle.

Set your sights on a place
Higher than your eyes can see.
For it was a higher aim
    that brought you here
    in the first place.

Now be silent.
Let the One who creates the words speak.
He made the door,
He made the lock,
    He also made the key.

Every question I ask is about you,
Every step I take is toward you.

I slept well last night
    but I woke up drunk.
I must have dreamt about you.

From Black Soot

What became of last night's promise?—
You broke it this morning!
But why should I care?
I can conquer the world with a blink,
    I can heal a broken heart with a smile.

O heart,
Make your wish—
The gifts are ready,
    the King is waiting with open arms.
The light of His Face
    is shining upon you.

I never heard a King say,
"Wait till tomorrow,
    then I'll give you everything."
Has dim light ever shown from the face of a full moon?

Where are the favors?
Where are the wise men?
Where are the open doors?
Where is the Revealer of Secrets?—
The answer is: "Right here!"
They are here, from the beginning to the end.
So it says,
    "You are what you seek."

Enough talk from me.
I have died at the Beloved's feet.
No, I am wrong—
One who gains life through Him
        can never die.

When the King's reflection dances upon the earth
Mud and stone come to life,
        brittle trees laugh,
        barren women give birth.

If His reflection can do this
Imagine what the light of His Face can do!
It is the brightness of every thought,
The light animating every soul,
The source of life
        from the Sun to the fourth heaven.

But one can only know the taste of salt
        by sprinkling it on his food.

What a wonder!
The Beloved is in love with the lover.
What a miracle!
From black soot grows a paradise.

You have two hands, two legs, and two eyes,
But if your heart and the Beloved are also two,
    what good is that?

You call out, *I am the lover,*
But these are mere words.
If you see lover and Beloved as two,
    you either have double vision
    or you can't count.

I've been dead to this world for a long time.
Every day my body grows weaker
    and soon it will return to the earth.
It's not difficult to renounce this life
    or this world,
But to give up your love,
    that is difficult—
    no, impossible.

The Breath of My Presence

I smell the fragrance of my Beloved
   and my heart is lost.
I see a ray of light from His face
   and my soul is enraptured.

Why are the earth and all its creatures
   bubbling up in delight?—
A drop from the *Saaqi's** cup
   has spilled upon the ground.

One who is frozen and withered
   is lost in his own affairs.
Don't be lost in your own affairs—
   be lost in mine!

The Spring reveals all the secrets of the earth.
My Spring reveals all the secrets of the soul.

The roses of the earth
   only hide the thorns and brambles.
When my roses bloom
   they remove every thorn from the heart.

What is the cold wind of winter?—
   the breath of your denial.
What is the warm breeze of Spring?—
   the breath that lets me into your life.

*Saaqi: *cupbearer, or one who pours wine; a symbol of God's grace. (See*
"Terms and Symbolism.")

Your Golden Cup

Here He comes—
A moon whose light the sky never saw
    even in her dreams,
Crowned with an eternal flame
    no flood can hope to quench.

His cup, long out of reach, now spills over,
    filling my senses,
    desolating my soul.

The *saaqi* has become my dearest friend.
With each new round she pours,
    my blood turns to nectar,
    my heart to a holy shrine.
Now I see only Him!
Now I hear His voice alone:

Let my love fill your golden cup
    like sunbeams showering the earth.
Let it flow to every corner of your soul,
Let it tear up the gnarled roots of regret
    and nourish the tender seeds of hope.

When my heart saw the ocean of His love
    it jumped in and yelled,
Find me if you can!

O, where can I look for my missing heart?
Where, but the face of Shams-e Tabriz? . . .

He is the Sun
In whose track
Every heart must follow.

My crippled poetry began to dance
    with the light of God's Name.

His Name brought the angel of words
    into the house of my mind.
In every verse a thousand maidens give birth,
    yet like Mary,
    each remains a virgin.

See that caravan of camels
    loaded up with sugar?—
His eyes contain that much sweetness.
But don't look into His eyes
    unless you're ready to lose all sight of your own.

One Lasting Truth

That awesome Beauty gives us everything.
Whose fault is it
    if we go away empty-handed?

Don't be disheartened
    if that Charmer is ruthless—
Who ever saw Him acting otherwise?

His love is sugar enough
    even when it gives no sugar.
His beauty is promise enough
    even when it causes you
    to break your promise.

    Show me a house where His light
        does not shine.
    Show me a garden where His grace
        does not bloom.

God was jealous of His own Face
    and so He created the splendor of morning.
When the spirit awoke in that light, it said,
    To grasp God's beauty, you must become God.

The eye and the lamp are different lights
    but when they come together
    no one can tell them apart.

What is true?
What is false?

The only truth I know in this world
    is my master, Shams-e Tabriz:
The light of his Sun
    has never shone upon anything passing
    without making it eternal.

All night I danced round the house of my Beloved.
In the morning he came out
    and offered me some wine.
I had no cup—
"Here's my empty skull," I said.
"Pour your wine in here."

O weary heart,
     the cure has finally come.
Draw in a sweet breath
     for the eternal moment has finally come.

The Beloved appears for the sake of His lovers—
Here, in a human form,
     he has finally come.

Wood for His Fire

If you don't have the Beloved
    why aren't you looking for Him?
If you have the Beloved
    why aren't you rejoicing?

If the Friend is truly your friend
Why not stay with Him?
If the rebec does not wail,
Why not teach it how to sing?
If someone bars you from the truth,
Why not fight him
    and his brother as well?

You sit quietly and say to yourself,
    "Something strange is going on."
The only thing strange
    is that your best friend is a stranger.

You are the Sun of the world—
Why is your heart so black?
Why do you fall back
    on your drab and stagnant ways?
Don't stay melted like gold in a furnace—
    Become a piece of jewelry!

The treasure of Unity is found
    by those who look within.
Why not join your spirit to the one
    who sits inside your heart?

Did Majnun ever love two Laylas?
Why seek more than one face and one cheek?

There is such a glorious moon
     hiding in the shadows of your being.
Why not make it rise
     with the power of a midnight prayer?
You have danced in the tavern for ages,
Love's wine never slips from your hand,
Yet with each new sip
     your soul is ravished like never before.

The wine I drink is the fire of love
And God Himself pours it into my mouth!

What use is your life
If your bones are not used
     as wood for His fire?

I'll leave you with that.
I could go on,
I could fill pages with these elegant verses
But this is a tale for the heart and soul,
     not the lips.

I knocked on the door
>of the One who embraces love.

He opened it, saw me there, and began to laugh.

He pulled me in—
>I melted like sugar cubes
>in the arms of that Lover, that Wizard of the World.

I'm in a daze—
    your wine overflows,
    sweetness falls from your lips.
O *Saaqi*,
    once you show yourself
    everything will be so clear.

When All You Had Was Him

O my Beloved,
I searched both worlds
    but never found joy without you.
I have seen many wonders
    but never a wonder like you.

I pressed my soul's ear
    against countless doors
But never heard words as sweet as yours.

    O what grace you pour upon your servants!
    From our view the ocean looks so small!

O *Saaqi,* sweet sight of my eyes,
I've never seen one like you
    in all of Persia or Arabia.
Pour the wine that takes me beyond myself,
    for this petty existence
    brings nothing but fatigue.

You are the endless Love,
You are the heavenly song,
You are the mother and father,
You are the one I will always know.

We are scraps of iron.
Your love is the magnet that draws us near.
Why should I seek?—
All I need do is love. . . .

Rest now my soul,
Leave behind your religion
    and your empty show of faith.

Remember when you had no religion?
Remember when all you had was Him?

Part Three

An
Endless
Celebration

Don't come to our party without a drum!
Stand up and play the melody,
 I am God—
That's all we want to hear.

And drink! Get drunk on the wine
 that cannot be found
 even in paradise.

The Roses Are in Bloom!

Come, come,
The roses are in bloom!
Come, come,
The Beloved has arrived!

Now is the time to unite
    the soul and the world.
Now is the time to see the sunlight
    dancing as one with the shadows.

Laugh at those faithless men
    who boast with loud voices.
Weep for that friend
    who has turned away from the Friend.

    The whole city is trembling with fear
        now that the madman
        has broken from his chains.

What a day!
What a day!
A day of upheaval!
A day of revolt!
Perhaps the scroll
    that records every deed
    is falling from the sky!

Beat the drum,
Speak no more—
The heart has gone,
The mind has gone,
The soul, too, has gone
    to the Beloved.

The seeds of His love blossom in every heart.
The sounds of His flute fill every celebration.
Everyone thinks that he sings and dances
But no—

    He is the only one singing,
    He is the only one dancing.

We drink the wine of our own blood,
	aged in the barrels of our souls.

We would give our lives for a sip of that nectar,
Our heads in exchange for one drop.

The Shepherd's Care

Join the community of saints
  and know the delight
  of your own soul.
Enter the ruins of your heart
  and learn the meaning of humility.

Drain the cup of passion
  and walk steadfast
  on the path of Truth.
Close both eyes
  and see the mysteries
  with your inner eye.

Open your arms if you want the Beloved's embrace.
Break your bonds with this body
  if you want to see
  His pure and radiant Face.

Would you marry an old woman
  to gain a dowry of a few pennies?
Would you face the threat of swords and spears
  for three loaves of bread?

The *Saaqi* is not a tyrant.
So come and sit within her circle.
How long will you stay outside
  and watch her dance
  the way you watch the circling night sky?

God's creation is vast—
Why do you sit all day in a tiny prison?

Look! He's giving you a real bargain—
Give up one and get a hundred.
Stop running around like a wolf or a dog—
    stay and receive the Shepherd's care.

You say, *He stole away my sweetheart!*
Forget it—twenty more sweethearts will come.

Thoughts of the Beloved will feed your soul.
How can your hunger be satisfied
    by thoughts of bread alone?

Speak little,
Learn the words of eternity.

Go beyond your tangled thoughts
    and find the splendor of Paradise.
Go beyond your little world
    and find the grandeur of God's world.

Walk by my grave and you'll become drunk.
Stand too long and your entire soul
     will become drunk.
Go to the ocean and all the waters
     will become drunk.
Die and be buried
     and all the earth will become drunk. . . .

And then, anyone who walks by *your* grave
     will become drunk.

On the Threshold

O lovers, O lovers,
    heaven's drum calls my spirit and says,
    It's time to leave this world.

Look!
The camel driver has risen,
The caravan is about to leave.
He says, "Forgive me for waking you. . . .
But why, O pilgrim, are you asleep?
Before you and behind you
    the camel-bells are ringing.
It's time to go."

With each passing moment
    a soul sets off to find itself.
From the stars,
    suspended like candles
    from the blue vault of heaven,
    wondrous souls have appeared
        and the Unseen has revealed itself.

The revolving spheres have lulled you
    into a deep sleep.
Beware of this floating life.
Beware of this weighty slumber.

O heart, seek the King of Hearts.
O friend, seek the Eternal Friend.

O watchman, be wakeful—
    the whole city could be lost
    if you fall asleep!

Tonight, amidst the shouts and din of the city,
Amidst the light of candles and torches—
Tonight this fecund world
    will give birth to eternity.

You were dust and now you are spirit.
You were ignorant and now you are wise.
The one who brought you here
    will bring you still further.
Your pain will become your pleasure
    as He draws you near.
Don't be afraid—
His flames are like cooling water.
To give your soul life is His sacred duty,
To break your binding chains is His only mission.

O foolish puppet, popping up from your box,
You call out to the world,
    This is mine!
How long will you jump up?
If you don't bend your neck
    He will bend it for you!

You put others down
    and spin a web of deception.
O imposter,
You think God is a plaything in your hand!

O donkey, you belong with the straw.
O cauldron, you deserve to be blackened!
O outcast,
    you deserve to be at the bottom of a well!

    "In me there's another force
    that gives rise to these harsh words.
    Scalding water
        is caused by fire, not water."

I have no stone in my hand,
    no argument with anyone.
I put down no one,
    for I am as sweet as a bed of roses.

That Supreme Source speaks through me. . . .
It has given you a hint—that is enough.

Now let me sit here,
    on the threshold of two worlds,
Lost in the eloquence of silence.

Don't turn from the delight
    that is so close at hand!
Don't find some lame excuse
    to leave our gathering.
You were a lonely grape
    and now you are sweet wine.
There is no use in trying to become a grape again.

The Birds of Paradise

Lovers of truth—rise up!
Let us go toward heaven.
We have seen enough of this world,
    it's time to see another. . . .

No, no—don't stop here.
The gardens may flow with beauty
But let us go to the Gardener Himself.

Let us go,
    bowing to the ocean
    like a raging torrent.
Let us go,
    riding upon the foaming waters
    of the sea.

Let us travel from this desert of
    hunger and tears
    to the feast of newlyweds.
Let us change our expression
    from one of saffron
    to the blossoms of the Judas tree.

Our hearts beat fast.
We tremble like leaves about to fall.
Let us become the immovable mountain.

There is no escape from pain for one in exile;
There is no escape from dust
    for one who lives in a dustbowl.
Let us be like the birds of paradise,
    that fly about drinking sweet water.

We are surrounded by the forms
    of a formless creator.
Enough with these forms!
Let us go to the Formless One.

Love is our steady guide
    on this road full of hardships.
Even if the king offers you his protection,
    it is better
    to travel with the caravan.

We are the rain that falls upon
    a leaky roof—
Let us miss the holes
    and fall smoothly down the spout.

We are crooked bows
    with strings that run from our head to our toes;
Soon we will be straight,
    like an arrow in flight.

We run like mice when we see a cat—
Yet we are the lion's roar.
Let us become that Lion.

Let our souls
    mirror the love of our Master.
Let us go before Him
    with a handful of gifts.

Now let us be silent
So that the Giver of Speech may speak.
Let us be silent
So we can hear Him calling us
    secretly in the night.

Our garden is filled with nightingales,
The crows have flown away.
Now we can see the flowers of your garden.

Like a lily we come out of ourselves,
Like a babbling brook
    we dance from one paradise to the next.

In the lover's heart is a lute
Which plays the melody of longing.

You say he looks crazy—
That's only because your ears are not tuned
    to the music by which he dances.

From self to Self

If a tree could run or fly
    it would not suffer from the teeth of a saw
    or the blows of an axe.
If the Sun did not run across the sky
    the world would not see
    the colors of morning.

If water did not rise from the sea
    plants would not be quickened
    by rivers or rain.
It's only when a drop leaves the ocean—and returns—
    that it can find an oyster
    and become a pearl.

When Joseph left his father
    both were weeping.
Didn't he gain a kingdom and a fortune
    in the end?
Didn't the Prophet
    gain the world and a hundred empires
    by traveling to Medina?

But you have no need to go anywhere—
    journey within yourself.
Enter a mine of rubies
    and bathe in the splendor of your own light.

O great one,
Journey from self to Self
  and find the mine of gold.
Leave behind what is sour and bitter—
  move toward what is sweet.
Be like the thousand different fruits
  that grow from briny soil.

This is the miracle—
Every tree becomes beautiful
  when touched by sunlight;
Every soul becomes God
  when touched by the Sun of Tabriz.

I want nothing to do with this world or the next,
Yet I do not turn away.

My own heart is filled with a million wonders.
Beholding this sight,
    what madness now keeps me
    from becoming totally mad?

We're not ahead, we're behind.
We' re not above, we're below. . . .

Like a brush in the painter's hand,
　we have no idea where we are.

Soft Petals

O soul,
Who dwells in the house of my heart?
Who takes the King's royal seat?

The King motions me forward and says,
What do you want from me?

I want the sweetness of love,
A cup of light,
An eternal banquet
on the table of one Truth.

Look how many charlatans are rattling their cups
at this wine-drinker's feast.
O simple and gullible man,
Watch out or you'll be conned!
Beware! Don't sit at their table
lest your eyes close like buds
and your mouth open like a Spring flower.

The world is but a mirror
reflecting Love's perfect image.
How can a part
be greater than the whole?
In this garden
only the Beloved's rose is blooming.
Stay low like the grass
and let His soft petals fall upon your head.

He is both the sword and the swordsman,
    the slayer and the slain.
He is reason
    and all that brings reason to naught.

That perfect King makes this world out of gold.
May he live forever.
May his hand be the ageless garland
    that graces my neck.

O heart,
Let go of all your worries about the future.
In this friendless world
    come and join *us.*

If you want to ride the horse
    that sails on the breeze of dawn
Then become the dust under the hoofs
    of a darvish's horse.

O tulip, come and learn
    the rainbow colors of my face.
O Venus, come and learn
    the notes of my heart.

When the music of union begins to play,
O destiny of a million lifetimes,
    come and learn its song!

Don't ask me about prayer rocks—
Anyplace I put my head is a prayer rock.
Don't talk of direction—
All six directions face Him.

Gardens, flames, nightingale,
    whirling dance, and brotherhood—
Throw all these away
    and throw yourself into His love.

Like This

If someone asks,
"What does perfect beauty look like?"
Show him your own face and say,
    Like this.

If someone asks,
"What does a full moon look like?"
Climb to the highest rooftop and yell,
    Like this.

If someone asks,
"What does an angel's wing look like?"—smile.
If he asks about divine fragrance
Pull him close, his face in your hair,
    Like this.

If someone asks,
"How did Jesus bring the dead back to life?"—
Don't say a word—
just kiss him softly on the cheek,
    Like this.

If someone asks,
"How does it feel to be slain by love?"
Close your eyes and tear open your shirt,
    Like this.

If someone asks about my stature,
Stare into space with your eyes wide open,
    Like this.

The soul enters one body, then another.
If someone argues about this
Enter my house and wave him good-bye,
    Like this.

Whenever a lover cries out
He is telling our story
And God bends down to listen,
    Like this.

I am the storehouse of all pleasure,
I am the pain of self-denial.
To see me, lower your eyes to the ground
Then raise them up to heaven,
    Like this.

Only the gentle breeze
Knows the secret of union.
Listen as it whispers a song to every heart,
    Like this.

If someone asks,
How does a servant attain the glory of God?
Become the shining candle
That every eye can see,
    Like this.

I asked about Joseph's perfume
Which rode the wind from city to city—
It was *your* scent
Blowing in from God's perfect world,
    Like this.

I asked how Joseph's perfume
Gave sight to the blind—
It was *your* breeze
Clearing the darkness from my eyes,
    Like this.

Perhaps Shams will be generous
And fill our hearts with love.
Perhaps he will raise one eyebrow
And cast us a glance,
    Like This.

Don't talk about night anymore!—
In our day there is no night.
In our religion of Love
    there is no religion or love.
Love is the endless ocean of God
Yet thousands of souls, drowning in that ocean, cry out—
    "There is no God!"

O eyes, rub your shirt in blood.
O soul, hang your clothes on the wheel
    of life and death.

O tongue, let the Lover sing.
O ears,
    get drunk on His song.

Don't Sleep

O seeker,
Listen to your heart's true yearning—
    Don't sleep!
Give up one night of your life to the vigil—
    Don't sleep!

You have spent a thousand nights
    in the cradle of sleep—
I ask for one night.
For the sake of the Friend,
    Don't sleep!
The Loving Witness never sleeps by night,
Follow *His* ways:
Give yourself to Him—
    Don't sleep!

Beware of that woeful night,
When you cry out in agony: "O God"—
    Don't sleep!
That night when Death comes to welcome you—
By the dread of that night, O weary one,
    Don't sleep!
Even stones will cry when bound
    by the weight of those chains.
You are not a stone.
Remember those chains—
    Don't sleep!

Though the night tempts you like a beautiful maiden,
    do not drink from her cup.
Fear the morning after—
    Don't sleep!

God says, "My dear ones will stay up with me at night."
If you hear these words,
    Don't sleep!

Fear that horrible night
    when no refuge can be found.
Store up your provisions tonight! Beware!
    Don't sleep!

The Saints find their treasure
    when the world is asleep;
For the sake of ever-giving love,
    Don't sleep!

When your spirit is old and worn
He will give you a new one,
Then you will become the pure spirit of all.
O hopeful one, don't sleep!

I have told you again and again—
    go to that inner silence!
    But still you do not hear me.

Give me one night
And I will give you a thousand in return—
    Don't sleep!

Part Four

The

Cauldron

of Love

O seeker,
These thoughts have such power over you.
From nothing you become sad,
From nothing you become happy.

You are burning in the flames
But I will not let you out
    until you are fully baked,
    fully wise,
    and fully yourself.

A Sacred Blasphemy

Be off and know
That the way of lovers is opposite all other ways.
Lies from the Friend
Are better than truth and kindness from others.

For Him
The impossible is commonplace,
Punishment is reward,
Tyranny is justice,
Slander is the highest praise.

His harshness is soft,
His blasphemy is sacred.
The blood that drips from the Beloved's thorn
    is sweeter than roses and basil.

When He's bitter
    it's better than a candy-shop.
When He turns his head away
    it's all hugs and kisses.
When He says, "By God, I've had enough of you!"
    it's like an eternal spring
    flowing from the fountain of life.

A "No" from his lips is a thousand times "Yes."
On this selfless path
    He acts like a stranger
    yet He's your dearest friend.

His infidelity is faith,
His stones are jewels,
His holding back is giving,
His ruthlessness is mercy.

You may laugh at me and say,
    "The path you're on is full of curves!"
Yes—for the curve of His eyebrow
    I have traded in my soul!

This curvy path has gotten me drunk,
I cannot say another word!
Carry on, my glorious heart,
    finish the poem in silence. . . .

O Shams, Lord of Tabriz,
What sweetness you pour upon me—
All I need do is open my mouth
    and all your songs flow out.

Every day my heart cries out,
Every night it turns to stone.

The story of my love
    is written in blood all over my face.
I ask my Beloved to read it.
He asks me to ignore it.

The mountain of your imagination
  amounts to no more than a few crumbs of bread.
All your coming and going
  was no more than an excuse.
For a lifetime
  you listened to the story of my heart,
But to you it was just a fairy tale.

He Gives to Taste

Do not despair
   if the Beloved pushes you away.
If He pushes you away today
   it's only so He can draw you back tomorrow.

If He closes the door on your face,
   don't leave, wait—
   you'll soon be by His side.
If He bars every passage,
   don't lose hope—
   He's about to show you
   a secret way that nobody knows.

A butcher cuts off a sheep's head for food,
   not just to throw away.
When the sheep no longer has breath
   the butcher fills it
   with his own breath.
O what life
   God's breath will bring to *you*!

But the likeness ends here—
For God's bounty is much greater than the butcher's.
God's blows don't bring death but eternal life.
He gives the wealth of Solomon to a single ant.
He gives the treasure of both worlds to all who ask.
He gives and gives
   yet does not startle a single heart.

I've traveled to all ends of the earth
    and have not found anyone like Him.
Who can match Him?
Who can hold a candle to His glory?

Silence already!
He gives us the wine to taste,
    not to talk about. . . .

He gives to taste.
He gives to taste.
He gives to taste.

When we were bound, He added another chain.
When we were suffering, He added another grief.
When we were lost in a house of mirrors
    He spun us round and round
    and added another mirror.

My face is yellow with regret—don't ask me why.
My tears are falling like the seeds of a pomegranate—
    don't ask me why.

Who cares what is going on inside my house?
There is blood on my doorstep—
    don't ask me why.

Who Is at My Door?

He said, "Who is at my door?"
  I said, "Your humble servant."
He said, "What business do you have?"
  I said, "To greet you, O Lord."

He said, "How long will you journey on?"
  I said, "Until you stop me."
He said, "How long will you boil in the fire?"
  I said, "Until I am pure.

  "This is my oath of love.
  For the sake of love
    I gave up wealth and position."

He said, "You have pleaded your case
    but you have no witness."
  I said, "My tears are my witness;
    the pallor of my face is my proof."
He said, "Your witness has no credibility;
    your eyes are too wet to see."
  I said, "By the splendor of your justice
    my eyes are clear and faultless."

He said, "What do you seek?"
  I said, "To have you as my constant friend."
He said, "What do you want from me?"
  I said, "Your abundant grace."

He said, "Who was your companion on the journey?"
I said, "The thought of you, O King."
He said, "What called you here?"
I said, "The fragrance of your wine."

He said, "What brings you the most fulfillment?"
I said, "The company of the Emperor."
He said, "What do you find there?"
I said, "A hundred miracles."
He said, "Why is the palace deserted?"
I said, "They all fear the thief."
He said, "Who is the thief?"
I said, "The one who keeps me from you."

He said, "Where is there safety?"
I said, "In service and renunciation."
He said, "What is there to renounce?"
I said, "The hope of salvation."

He said, "Where is there calamity?"
I said, "In the presence of your love."
He said, "How do you benefit from this life?"
I said, "By keeping true to myself."

Now it is time for silence.
If I told you about His true essence
You would fly from your self and be gone,
    and neither door nor roof could hold you back!

The secret Heart-Ravisher has been exposed!
I have found traces of his footsteps all around.

If He is not God, He is the one sent by God.

O musician of my soul,
    play His song
    play His song with every breath.

I said,
"O sweet Beloved,
    you are the refuge of my soul."
He said, "If you belong to me,
    don't talk of your own soul."
I said, "Why do you cut me
    with your sharp words?"
He said, "My words wouldn't hurt you
    if you weren't in love with yourself."

I Cried Out at Midnight

I cried out at midnight,
    "Who lives in the house of my heart?"
An answer came back,
    "It is I, whose radiance
    puts the Sun and Moon to shame."

He then asked,
"Why is this house of the heart
    so full of images?"
I said, "They are the reflections of you,
    whose face is the envy of Chigil."
He asked, "What is this other image
    all soaked in blood?"
I said, "It is me
    with my heart torn open
    and my feet caught in the mud."

I tied a noose round the neck of my soul
    and brought it to Him:
"Here is the one who turned his back on love—
    Do not let him escape this time."

He gave me one end of a thread
    which was twisted with guile and deceit.
He said, "Pull on this end,
I will pull on the other,
And let's hope the thread doesn't break
    in the pulling."

From the chamber of my soul
    the form of my Beloved
    shone more radiant than ever.
I reached out and grabbed Him with my hand—
    He knocked it away and said,
"Don't cling to me!"
I said, "You've become harsh like all the rest."

He said, "Don't insult me—I am harsher than all the rest!
But what I do is born of love, not malice or spite.
I am here to make your heart a shrine of love,
    not a pen for holding sheep. . . ."

The Beautiful One has made this world out of gold.
Rub your eyes and see
    that He is the keeper of your heart.

O flute,

> *You have no tongue, yet you wail all day?*
> *For whom do you cry?*

The flute said:

> *They took me from His sweet lips.**
> *What else can I do but cry?*

**The flute, cut from the reed bed, symbolizes a soul cut off from its own
source, the lover cut off from the Beloved.*

I dreamt that the Beloved entered my body,
    pulled out a dagger,
    and went looking for my heart—
He couldn't find it.
So he struck anywhere.

I woke up
    counting this as a blessing.

He said, *I'll turn you round like a treadmill,*
　　I'll make your head spin,
　　I'll turn your life into ruins.

I said, *Well then, I'll find someone else.*
He said, *Who?*—
　　If you find someone else
　　I'll make it even worse for you.

My King

I was dead and now I am alive.
I was in tears and now I am laughing.
The power of love swept over my soul
    and now I am that eternal power.

My eyes are content.
My soul is fulfilled.
My heart is roaring.
My face glows like Venus.

He said, "But you are not mad with love.
    You don't belong in this house."
I went and became mad.
I put chains round my neck.

He said, "But you are not drunk with love.
    You don't belong at this party."
I went and became drunk.
I rolled on the floor with joy.

He said, "But you have not tasted the sweetness of death."
I sipped the wine of death
    and fell before His life-giving face.

He said, "But you are a worldly man,
    you have so many clever questions."
I went and became a fool,
    babbling at every street-corner. . . .

He said, "Now you are a candle.
Everyone in the gathering has turned toward you."

   "No, I don't belong here.
   I am not a candle,
   I am a wisp of smoke."

He said, "You are a Shaykh and a Master,
A guide of lost souls."

   "No, I am not a Shaykh nor a guide,
   I am slave to your every word."

He said, "You can fly.
Why should I give you feathers and wings?"

   "For *your* feathers and wings
   I would clip my own
         and crawl upon the ground. . . ."

You are the majestic fountain of the Sun
      that pours upon my head.
I am the shadow of a willow tree
      bent over and melting.

When my heart was warmed by your radiant Sun
I took off my torn clothes
      and put on fine silk.
My soul was once a slave and a donkey-driver,
Now it swaggers down the street
      like a kingly lord.

The knowledge of you has lifted me up,
Now I am a star shining above the seventh heaven.
I was a glitter in the night sky,
Now I am the Moon and the two hundred folds of heaven.
I was Joseph at the bottom of a well,
Now I am Joseph the King!

O famous Moon, shine on me.
A ray of your light
    would turn my world into a rosegarden.

Now I will move in silence,
Like a chess piece,
Watching as my whole life
    revolves around
    the position of my King.

You have made me weary
    yet the bitterness of your torment
    is nectar to my heart.

I cannot complain about this pain—
But as long as you're listening,
    I'll tell you the whole story.

Blood from the heart of lovers
    will run as deep as a mighty river.
The lovers will be like bubbles in that torrent of blood.

Your body is a mill wheel and love is the water.
Have you ever seen a mill wheel turn without water?

Love Tricks

Who is this Beautiful One,
This One who stays up all night
    teaching love tricks to Venus and the Moon?
This One
    whose enchanting gaze
    seals up the two eyes of heaven?

O seekers, it is your own heart!

Day and night,
I am so taken by Him
    that no one else can be taken by me.
At the beginning I was born of His love,
In the end I gave Him my heart.
A fruit which falls from a branch
    must first cling to that same branch.

A man may run from his own shadow,
    searching for light,
      but will he ever find a place to rest?

The tip of His curl is saying,
    "Walk this tightrope."
The fire of His candle is saying,
    "O moth, come here."
O heart, be steady,
    dance gently upon that rope.

But the moment you hear His call
 fly into the candle's flame.

When you knew the rapture of this burning
 you would not go on for another moment
 without its heat.
Even if the water of life
 were pouring all around
 it would not lure you from the flames.

When I shed tears of blood
   you made me laugh.
When I was gone from this world
   you brought me back.
Now you ask,
What about your promises?
What promises?—
   you made me break them all.

O precious soul,
    this longing will make you pure.
O sacred body,
    this longing will make you thin.

O great one,
The fire of love that you burn in
Will turn your world into paradise.

Part Five

A
Mine of
Rubies

A Mine of Rubies

Last night I learned how to be a lover of God,
To live in this world and call nothing my own.

I looked inward
And the beauty of my own emptiness
    filled me till dawn.
It enveloped me like a mine of rubies.
Its hue clothed me in red silk.

Within the cavern of my soul
I heard the voice of a lover crying,
"Drink now! Drink now!"—

I took a sip and saw the vast ocean—
Wave upon wave caressed my soul.
The lovers of God dance around
And the circle of their steps
    becomes a ring of fire round my neck.

Heaven calls me with its rain and thunder—
a hundred thousand cries
yet I cannot hear. . . .

All I hear is the call of my Beloved.

Inner Sunrise

If I were the plaything of every thought
I'd be a fool, not a wise man.
If the Sun of Love was not my own
I'd be mournful like Saturn,
     rising and falling in the night sky.

If I were not guided by the fragrance of Love's City
I'd have followed dark spirits
     into the endless desert of greed.

If the soul's light had to stay inside its house
     I'd open every door and window!

If the garden of the soul
     did not comfort those in pain
     I could not carry Love's message
     on the east wind.

If lovers were not addicted to music and dancing
     why would I sing all day and night
     like a wailing flute?

If the *Saaqi's* weight-giving wine
     had been kept from my mouth
     I'd be like the thin lip of a cup!

If the Garden had no leaves or shade
     I'd be rootless
     like the fortune-trees of deceitful men.

If God's servants were not upon the earth
    I'd have fallen into the sin
    and folly of this world.

If there was no way from the grave to paradise
    I could not behold the joyful heavens
    in this body.

If there was no road from East to West
    I would not be dancing through the garden
    with the North and South winds!

If the Abundant Garden did not grow
    my soul would never blossom.
If God's grace were not with me
    I'd be a babbling fool!

Go within.
Hear the story of sunrise from the Sun itself.
If there were no sunrise within
    I would have set long ago!

When you move around Saturn, you become the heavens.
When you move around the Men of God,
     you become a true man.
When you move around a mine,
     you become a ruby.
When you move around the Soul of souls
     you become that eternal treasure.

The Dome of the Inner Sky

The Great King is within me.
He is my dearest friend.

Don't look at my sallow face,
Look at how I stand with legs of iron!—
Always turning toward that One
   who gave me life.

I am the glorious Sun,
   the ocean laden with pearls.
Within my heart is the grandeur of heaven,
Outside, the lowly earth.

I travel in this world like a bee in a jar.
But don't listen to my woeful buzzing—
My house is filled with honey!

O heart, if you want to join us,
   raise yourself
    to the dome of the inner sky.
Enter the fortress that no one can break.

The vast and mighty waters
   move the grinding stones of heaven.
I am that great wheel,
   crying so sweetly,
    turning with the flow of rushing water.

Men, demons, and spirits all follow my command.
Can't you see that I am Solomon,
    with a shimmering seal on my ring?

Why should I be weary
    when every cell of my body is bursting with life?
Why should I be a donkey's slave
    when I ride upon a magical horse?
Why should I be less than the Moon
    when there are no scorpions at my feet?
Why should I stay at the bottom of a well
    when a strong rope is in my hand?

I've built a place for the falcons of my soul—
Fly this way, O birds of spirit,
    for I am surrounded by a hundred mighty towers!

I am the rays of the Sun
    dancing through the windows of every house.
I am carnelian, gold, and rubies,
    even though this body is made of water and clay.

Whatever pearl you seek,
    look for the pearl within the pearl!

The surface of the earth says,
    "The treasure is within."
The glowing jewel says,
    "Don't be fooled by my beauty—
    the light of my face
    comes from the candle of my spirit."

What else can I say?
You will only hear
 what you are ready to hear.
Don't nod your head,
Don't try to fool me—
 the truth of what you see
 is written all over your face!

This Eternal Play

At dawn the Moon appeared in the sky.
It floated down and looked at me.
Then, like a hawk snatching its prey,
　　it grabbed hold of me
　　and dragged me across the sky.

When I looked I could not see myself.
By the magic of the Moon's light
　　my body dissolved into pure spirit.
In this form I journeyed on
Merging with a boundless light.
Then the secret of this eternal play
　　opened up before me.

The nine spheres of heaven
　　were enveloped in light.
The ship of my soul
　　was lost in a shoreless Sea. . . .

Suddenly the Sea of Being formed into waves.
Thoughts rose up,
　　images and forms broke on the shore.
Then everything returned to the way it was before,
　　merging into that vast Spirit.

The fortune of this sight
　　comes from Shams, the Truth of Tabriz.
Without his grace,
　　no one could ever ride the Moon
　　or become the endless Sea.

Like a flower's sweet nectar,
    you were born laughing.
The planets say
    you will be the happiest man in the world.
You are graceful like the stem of a flower
    and free like the towering cypress.

But there is something very strange
    about this cypress—
It's flying!

Willing Slaves

From deep within my heart
I always catch
    the scent of my Beloved.
How can I help but
    follow that fragrance?

Last night I was walking through Love's garden
    where a glimmer of my soul
    became a teeming river of light!
Laughing roses sprang up along the banks.
Dazzling waters rolled past the thorns of being
    with speed enough to elude the sword of death.
Every tree and blade of grass danced in the meadow.
But to an eye without this vision,
    all seemed plain and ordinary.
Suddenly a great cypress shot up from the ground!
The whole garden roared with delight—
    the jasmines exploded,
    the broad-leafed trees clapped their hands.

A face of fire,
A cup of fire,
A heart of fire—
    all were blazing with joy.
Surrounded by flames, my soul called out,
    O God, where shall I run?

In the world of Oneness
    there is nothing but yourself,
    there is no room for counting.
But in the world of things
    there is so much counting.
You may count a thousand apples in your hand—
If you want them all to be one,
    make applesauce.
You may count a thousand grapes in your hand—
If you want the precious wine
    crush them all together.

The message behind the words
    is the voice of the heart.
The source of all activity
    is that utter stillness.

Now Shams-e Tabriz is in the royal seat
    and all my rhymes
    have lined up like willing slaves.

The Glitter of This Fantasy

Now comes the final merging,
    Now comes everlasting beauty.
Now comes abundant grace,
    Now comes boundless purity.

The infinite treasure is shining,
The mighty ocean is roaring,
The morning of grace has come—
Morning?—No!
This is the eternal Light of God!

Who occupies this beautiful form?
Who is the ruler and the prince?
Who is the wise man?—
    Nothing but a veil.

The wine of love removes these veils.
Drink with your head and your eyes—
Both your eyes,
And both your heads!

Your head of clay is from the earth,
Your pure awareness is from heaven.
O how vast is that treasure
    which lies beneath the clay!
Every head you see depends on it!

Behind every atom of this world
hides an infinite universe.

O Saaqi, free us from the façade of this world.
Bring wine—barrels full!
Our eyes see too straight—
straight past the truth!

The Light of Truth shines from Tabriz.
It is beyond the beyond
yet it is here,
shining through every particle of this world.

Your heart is the size of an ocean—
Go find the gem hidden in your depths!

Your open mouth cries like a seashell:
    That heart is too small for me!
That heart contains the whole universe,
How could it be too small for you?

You searched the whole world for life
    yet in your own heart you will die.
You were born in the blissful arms of union
    yet alone you will die.

You have fallen asleep by the edge of a lake
    and now you are thirsty.
You sit on top of a treasure
    yet in utter poverty you will die.

Throw Down Your Staff

I saw that good and beautiful King,
That Witness of the heart's light,
That comforter and friend of the soul,
That spirit of all the world.

I saw the One who gives
    wisdom to the wise,
    purity to the pure;
The one adorned by the Moon and stars,
The one toward whom all saints bow.

    Every cell of my body called out,
    Praise God! Glory to God!

When Moses saw the radiant fire of the bush, he said:
After finding this gift I need nothing more.

God said, *O Moses, your wandering is over.*
    Throw down your staff.
In that moment Moses cast from his heart
    all friends, relatives, and kinsmen.

This is the meaning of "Take off both your shoes"—
    Remove from your heart the desire of both worlds.
The abode of the heart has room for God alone.
You will know this through the grace of the prophets.

God said, *O Moses, what do you hold in your hand?*
Moses replied, *This is my rod for the journey.*

God said,
    Throw it down and behold the marvels within yourself!
Moses tossed his rod to the ground
    and it became a serpent.
When Moses saw the serpent he ran in fear.

God said,
*Pick it up and I will turn it
    into a staff once again.*
Through my grace your foes will grant you blessings,
Your enemies will reach out in friendship.
When We bring suffering to your hands and feet
    like the burning pain of snake-bites—carry on.

O hand, keep reaching for Us.
O feet, keep walking toward the Goal!
Do not run from the hardship We give you,
For wherever you find hardship,
    you will also find the means to its end.

No one has ever escaped from hardship
    without something worse happening in return.

Don't take the bait!—
It will only lead to disaster.
Don't give in to your doubts!—
It will shake you from your ground.

Now Shams has shown us his mercy—
He went away
    and left us with nothing but ourselves.

A poet I am not!
My verses aren't worth
a piece of bread.
I don't seek praise,
I don't run from blame—
both are worthless to me.

All my skill and poetry
fit into a single cup—
Unless the wine comes from the Beloved's hand
I will not drink one sip of it!

The Bread of Egypt

My poetry is like the bread of Egypt—
    if one night passes
    it will become stale.
Partake while it is still fresh,
    before it dries out in the air.

My words rise in the warmth of the heart,
    they fade in the cold of the world.
Like fish on dry land
    they quiver for a moment, then die.

If you take in my words but do not digest them
    you'll have to color every truth
    with your own imaginings.

O man, you drink from an empty cup
    while the precious wine gets poured
    in the gutter.
You drink from the well of your own delusion
    while spitting out
    these sweet and ancient words.

If you eat stale bread
    thinking that it's fresh,
    all you'll get is a stomachache.

A Lover Without a Tear

One who does not have the Beloved
  is like a person without a head.
One who flees the cage of love
  is like a bird without wings.

What news could one have of the world
That the Keeper of Secrets does not have?

One who is pierced by the arrows of his glance
  is like a warrior without a shield.

One who cannot look within himself
  is like a man without valor.
One who can't open the door of his own heart
  is like a lover without a tear.

  He has placed a door
  In the middle of this path.
  Only He who has placed it
    can open it.

They say, "Wake up, the dawn has come!"
But in our sky who sleeps?
  Who gets up at dawn?
Our sky
  is without a sunrise
  and without a sunset.

You've only been here a few days
    and you've become so friendly with life.
I can't even talk about death anymore.

You're on the journey home
And your donkey has fallen asleep
    in the middle of the road!

No Place to Hide

When I set out, he is my goal.
When I look in my heart, he is its ravisher.
When I seek justice, he is the judge.
When I go to war, he is my weapon.

When I join the celebration,
He is the wine and sweetmeats.
When I enter the garden,
He is the narcissus in bloom.

When I go into a mine,
He is the ruby and carnelian.
When I dive into the ocean,
He is the pearl at the bottom.

When I cross the desert,
He is the watering hole.
When I rise to the spheres,
He is the brightest star.

When I show my courage,
He is the shield.
When I burn from heartache,
He is the incense holder.

When I fight a battle,
He is the commander-in-chief.
When I enter the banquet hall,
He is the *saaqi,* the minstrel, and the cup.

When I write to my friends,
He is the pen and the paper.
When I need a rhyme for a poem,
He gives me the right clue.

When I awake
He is my pure awareness.
When I go to sleep
He is the one who plays in my dreams.

Whatever picture you paint
    or poem you write
    he is beyond that.
Whatever height you can reach,
    he is higher than your "highest."

Get rid of your talking and your books—
    it is far better
    to let *Him* be your book.

See his light fill the heavens.
And when you pass beyond the heavens
    you'll find him hiding there.

O Wondrous Light of Tabriz,
Where will you hide?—
The brilliance of your Sun,
    will always give you away.

Prince of Eternity

O Prince,
    with your tiny horse and saddle,
You're a charlatan! A knave!
Though your head is bound in gold cloth
Your eyes see only what they want to see.

You say, "Where is death? I don't see death!"
Death will greet you from all six directions
    and say, "Here I am."
Death will say,
    "O donkey, your running about is over."
Where is your moustache, your pride,
    your turned-up nose?—Gone.
Where is your beautiful maiden?— Gone.
Where is your glimmer of happiness?—Gone.
Who will come to make your bed
    now that your pillow is a brick
    and your blanket is the earth? . . .

Say good-bye to your eating and sleeping.
Go and seek the truth within.
Throw away your petty rituals
    and become a prince of eternity.

Don't take the soul from your soul.
Don't turn this bread into poison.
Can't you see?—
    Someone has tossed a pearl
    into the bottom of a dung heap.

It is only for the sake of that pearl
     that we cover our hands with dung.

O soul,
Don't be so hard—break!
Find a lustrous pearl
     among the broken shells
     of your pride.

When you see a man of God
     offer him your service.
When you are troubled and in pain
     just keep going. . . .

O body, what a joke!—
The Prince I'm looking for is me
     yet I spend all my time
     thinking I am you!

O Shams, Lord of Tabriz,
You are the water of life—
Who shall drink of your water,
     save one with a tearful eye?

Don't be like a sparrow
　　jumping from branch to branch.
While you look for love here and there
The fire I lit inside you
　　will only grow cold.

The face of your religion
    covers the face of His Love.
You are like a donkey
    that carries sugar candy on its back
    but cannot taste it.

If a mirror shows you your own ugliness
    what is the use
    of breaking the mirror with your fist?

Lies!

◆

They say,
"The King of Love will turn from His lovers."—Lies!
They say, "The darkness will never turn to dawn."—Lies!

They say, "Do not sacrifice your life for love's sake.
When the body dies, you will die."—Lies!

They say, "The tears you shed in love are worthless.
They block your eyes and hold you from the truth."—
     Lies!

They say, "You can go beyond the cycle of time
     but your soul can travel no further."—Lies!

People who are caught in their own vanity say,
"The lives of the prophets are nothing but fairy tales."—
     Lies!

People who have lost their way say,
"The servant can never reach God."—Lies!

They say,
"The Knower of Secrets does not tell His
     servants all the mysteries of the Unseen."—Lies!

They say,
"He does not reveal the heart's innermost secrets.
He does not lift His servants up to heaven."—Lies!

They say, "One who is born of Earth
    will never join the angels of heaven."—Lies!

They say, "The pure soul must remain in this earthly nest;
    it will never soar on the wings of love."—Lies!

They say, "The Sun of God does not fill this whole world;
He misses a few atoms."—Lies!

Now go to that inner stillness.
Some say, "You will not hear the voice of God there."—
    Lies!

Only Through This

Abandon this world
That you may become King of all worlds.
Throw away your handful of sugar
That you may become a sugar field.

Leap like a flame through the sky.
Scatter the dark spirits
and become the pillar of heaven.

When Noah sails upon the flooding waters
you will be his ark.
When the Prophet ascends to heaven
you will be his ladder.
When Jesus walks among the weary souls
you will be his healing breath.
When Moses goes forth as a shepherd
you will be his staff.

A divine fire blazes within you.
Don't jump back like a coward.
Cook in that fire!
Bake like bread!
Soon you'll be the prize of every table,
the life-giving food of every soul.

Walk patiently through this troubled world
and you'll find a great treasure.
Even though your house is small, look within it—
you will find the secrets
of the unseen world.

I asked, "Why have I received only this?"
A voice replied,
     "'Only this' will lead you to That!"

No more words from my mouth.
I didn't come here to wag my chin,
I came here to chew on sugar-cane.

The Black Cloud

Lose yourself,
Lose yourself in this love.
When you lose yourself in this love,
    you will find everything.

Lose yourself,
Lose yourself.
Do not fear this loss,
For you will rise from the earth
    and embrace the endless heavens.

Lose yourself,
Lose yourself.
Escape from this earthly form,
For this body is a chain
    and you are its prisoner.
Smash through the prison wall
    and walk outside with the kings and princes.

Lose yourself,
Lose yourself at the foot of the glorious King.
When you lose yourself
    before the King
    you will become the King.

Lose yourself,
Lose yourself.
Escape from the black cloud
    that surrounds you.
Then you will see your own light
    as radiant as the full moon.

Now enter that silence.
This is the surest way
    to lose yourself. . . .

What is your life about, anyway?—
    Nothing but a struggle to be someone,
    Nothing but a running from your own silence.

Who said the eternal one has died?
Who said the Light of hope has died?
The enemy of the Sun is on the rooftop.
With his eyes closed he yells out,
    "The brilliant Sun has died!"

I Am a Painter

I am a painter,
Painting pictures all the time,
Yet when I set them near your beauty
I want to throw them all away.

I am a sculptor, carving images
    and filling each with life,
Yet when I compare these with your beauty
    I want to dump them in a fire.

O bringer of sweet wine,
Enemy of the sober,
You have laid waste to
    every house I ever built!

My soul has merged with yours—
Water into water, wine into wine.
Now there is only love
    and the scent of your rose perfume.

Every drop of my blood calls out,
    Dye me with the color of your love.
    Make me the jewel of your affection.

In this house of water and clay
    my heart is in ruins.
O Beloved, don't leave this house
    else it will crumble to the ground.

Better than Cabbage Soup

What sweetness lies in an empty stomach!
Man is like a lute—no more, no less.
If the lute is full
    it cannot sing a high or low note.

If your mind and stomach
    burn with the fire of hunger
    it will be like a heavenly song for your heart.
In each moment that fire rages
It will burn away a hundred veils
And carry you a thousand steps
    toward your goal.

Be empty
    and weep with the fullness of the reed flute.
Be empty
    and discover the mysteries of the reed pen.

If your belly is full on the day you are called
    pain will come instead of freedom,
    worldly cares will come instead of paradise.
When you fast, good qualities will gather round you
    like faithful friends and servants.

Don't break the fast
    for it is Solomon's Seal.
Don't give the Seal to harmful spirits.
Don't destroy your kingdom with a full belly.

Even if your kingdom falls
    and your armies abandon you,
    keep the fast.
Soon they will return
    with their banners high in the air.
I say, by the prayer of Jesus,
    Heaven's Table will come to your fasting tent.

Fast and remember that the abundance
    of Heaven's Table will soon be yours—
And I assure you,
    the food on that Table
    is better than cabbage soup!

O soul,
Could I ever turn from you?—No way!
Could I ever fall in love
    with anyone else?—No way!
In the garden of your love
    All I see are the flowers in bloom.
Could I ever turn toward the thorns?—No way!

Hold to the reins of Love and don't be afraid.
Hold to the real behind the false and don't be afraid.

You must know
    that the Beloved you seek is none other than you.
Hold to this truth and don't be afraid.

Through an Open Window

◆

Come here and catch a kiss
    from those ruby lips.
And if it costs you your life,
    consider it a bargain!

But that kiss is too pure to mix with dust—
You must become a floating spirit,
    free from this body.

The Ocean of Purity said to me:
    Nothing is attained without effort.
    To get the precious pearl
        you must first smash the shell.

For the rose's kiss
This whole world is parching its lily-lips.

I dare say,
Even if you have the splendor of every king,
And the beauty of Mars and Venus,
    don't accept a kiss
    from that beguiling Maiden.

O Moon of the dark sky—come in.
    I have opened the window for you.
Tonight, touch my face,
    press your lips upon mine.

Close the door of words
    that the window of your heart may open—
The Moon's kiss
    only comes
    through an open window.

A Ball of Wax

O lovers! O lovers!—
I can turn dust into diamonds!
O minstrels! O minstrels!
I can fill your tambourines with gold!

O thirsty souls! O thirsty souls!
I can give you water to drink,
I can turn this dustbin
    into the flowing waters of paradise!

O beggar! O beggar!
Your desperate call is over.
I can turn your aching heart
    into the King's crown!

O love! O love!
Pour down on this world.
I can turn every ruin into a mosque,
    every gallows into a pulpit.

O skeptics! O skeptics!
I can open your heart!
I can pull the strings
    that turn people toward doubt or faith.

O braggers! O braggers!
You are a ball of wax in my hand!
Become a sword
    and I will turn you into a cup.
Become a cup
    and I will turn you into a sword.

You began as a drop of semen,
   then you became blood.
Now you have attained this wonderful form.
Come to me, O son of Adam,
   I will make you even more beautiful.

I can turn sorrow into joy,
I can turn a wild beast into Joseph,
I can turn poison into nectar,
I can find all those who have gone astray.

O *Saaqi!* O *Saaqi!*
My mouth is open wide.
Let every dry mouth
   be joined to the lip of your cup.

O garden! O garden!
Let me use your roses for my rosary
   and I will let your flowers bloom in my heart.

O Heaven! O Heaven!
You'll be more confused than the narcissus
   when I change dust into ambergris,
      thorns into jasmine.

O Wisdom! O Wisdom!
You are the King of Truth
   who offers a treasure to all those who ask.
Why should I say another word?—
What could I add to your endless giving?

In Silence

A guide has entered this life in silence.
His message is only heard in silence.

Take a sip of his precious wine
And lose yourself.
Don't insult the greatness of his love,
For he helps all those who suffer, in silence.

Polish the mirror between the breaths.
Go with him, beyond words.
He knows your every deed.
He is the one
    who moves the wheel of heaven, in silence.

Every thought is buried in your heart;
He will reveal them one by one, in silence.

Turn each of your thoughts into a bird
And let them fly to the other world.
One is an owl, one is a falcon, one is a crow.
Each one is different from the others
But they are all the same in silence.

To see the Moon that cannot be seen
Turn your eyes inward
    and look at yourself, in silence.

In this world and the next,
Don't talk about this and that;
Let him show you everything,
    shining as one . . . in silence.

Part Six

The
Bliss
of
Union

Your Triumphant Song

On that final day
When my casket moves along
Do not think my soul
   will stay in this world.

Do not weep for me, crying, *Tragedy, tragedy.*
You will only fall into the snares of delusion—
   Now that's a tragedy!

When you see my lifeless body go by
Do not cry out, *Gone, gone.*
It is my moment of union.
It is when I come upon
   the eternal embrace of my Beloved.

As I am lowered into the ground
Do not say, *Farewell, farewell.*
For the grave is but a veil
   covering the splendor of Paradise.

   Having seen the fall
   Consider the rise.
   What harm ever came to the setting Sun or Moon?

What appears to you as a setting
   is for me a rising.
What appears to you as a prison
   is for my soul an endless garden.

Every seed that enters the earth will grow.
Should it be any different with a human seed?
Every bucket that is lowered into a well comes up full.
Should I complain when instead of water
    I pull up Joseph himself?

Do not look for your words here,
    look for them over there.
Sing to me in the silence of your heart
    and I will rise up
        to hear your triumphant song.

The secrets of eternity are beyond us
And these puzzling words
    we cannot understand.
Our words and actions take place
    on this side of the veil.

O soul,
When the veil is gone, we are gone.

With every breath I plant the seeds of devotion—
I am a farmer of the heart.

Day and night I see the face of union—
I am the mirror of God.

Every moment I shape my destiny with a chisel—
I am the carpenter of my own soul.

The Blast of That Trumpet

Remember me.
I will be with you in the grave
    on the night you leave behind
    your shop and your family.
When you hear my soft voice
    echoing in your tomb,
    you will realize
    that you were never hidden from my eyes.
I am the pure awareness within your heart,
    with you during joy and celebration,
    suffering and despair.

On that strange and fateful night
    you will hear a familiar voice—
    you'll be rescued from the fangs of snakes
    and the searing sting of scorpions.
The euphoria of love will sweep over your grave;
    it will bring wine and friends, candles and food.

When the light of realization dawns,
    shouting and upheaval
    will rise up from the graves!
The dust of ages will be stirred
    by the cries of ecstasy,
    by the banging of drums,
    by the clamor of revolt!

Dead bodies will tear off their shrouds
and stuff their ears in fright—
What use are the senses and the ears
before the blast of *that* Trumpet?

Look and you will see my form
whether you are looking at yourself
or toward that noise and confusion.

Don't be blurry-eyed,
See me clearly—
See my beauty without the old eyes of delusion.

Beware! Beware!
Don't mistake me for this human form.
The soul is not obscured by forms.
Even if it were wrapped in a hundred folds of felt
the rays of the soul's light
would still shine through.

Beat the drum,
Follow the minstrels of the city.
It's a day of renewal
when every young man
walks boldly on the path of love.

Had everyone sought God
Instead of crumbs and copper coins
They would not be sitting on the edge of the moat
in darkness and regret.

What kind of gossip-house
    have you opened in our city?
Close your lips
    and shine on the world
    like loving sunlight.

Shine like the Sun of Tabriz rising in the East.
Shine like the star of victory.
Shine like the whole universe is yours!

The Ashes of Union

O Soul,
You are the Phoenix
    rising up from the ashes of Union.
Why don't you fly?—
No one knows you on the ground.

You are the heart's sweetness
And by some magical power
    your form ravishes a thousand hearts.

For a time you took form in the body.
For a time you passed beyond the heavens
    and the bonds of both worlds.

Why can't the spirit find you?—
You are its wings and its feathers.
Why can't the eye see you?—
You are the source of its sight.

What will happen to your copper soul
    when the Alchemist arrives?—
Will it not become gold?
What will become of your little seed
    when the Springtime arrives?—
Will it not become a towering tree?
What will happen to brushwood
    when it falls into fire?—
Will it not change into sparks and rise to heaven?

Reason and intellect
Are like the dim light of distant stars.
You are the bright Sun
that shines through every veil.

The world is nothing but snow and ice.
You are the burning heat of Summer.
O King, no trace of this world remains
the moment you arrive!

Who can sit by your side?
Everyone would vanish with one glance of yours.

O blessed eyes!
I have seen something beyond imagination,
unreachable by fortune or human effort—
I have seen the perfect face
of Shams-e Tabriz.

I said, *This longing in my heart*
is more a curse than a cure.

He said, *What is your cure?*
I said, *Union.*
He said, *And what is my cure?*
I said, *Union.*

In their seeking,
    wisdom and madness are one and the same.
On the path of love,
    friend and stranger are one and the same.

Once you taste the wine of union
    what will be your faith?—
You'll tell everyone
    that the Ka'be and the idol temple*
    are one and the same.

*The Ka'be is the most sacred place of worship for Muslims; it is the
cube-shaped shrine in Mecca that all worshippers face while praying. The
idol temple (where idols are worshipped) is regarded as the lowest place.
This attitude stems from the fierce Judaic tradition that regards idol
worship as blasphemy.

Master San'ai

Someone said, "Master San'ai is dead."

The death of such a master is no small thing.
He was not chaff blown about by the wind,
Nor a puddle frozen over in winter.
He was not a comb broken in the hair,
Nor a seed crushed on the ground.

He was a piece of gold in a pile of dust.
The value he put on both worlds
    was equal to one barleycorn.

He let his body fall back into the earth
    and bore the witness of his soul to heaven.
But there is a second soul
    of which common men are not aware.
I tell you before God,
That one merged straight with the Beloved!

What was once mixed is now separate:
The pure wine rose to the top,
The dregs settled to the bottom.

During their travels, everyone walks together—
    people from Marv and Rayy, the Kurds and Romans.
But soon each returns to his homeland.
How can fine silk stay bound to rough wool?

He has reached the final stage.
The King has erased his name
    from the book of words. . . .

O Master, now that you're gone from this world,
How can we reach you
    but in silence?

In this world of love
    we are the hidden treasure,
    we are the owners of eternity.

The love affair with this body is over.
Having tasted the water of life
We've become the immortal Sufi.

The living word of pure Consciousness—you are That.
The reflection of the King's Face—you are That.
There is nothing outside of yourself,
    Look within,
Everything you want is there—you are That.

Pure Light

I am totally lost in the folds of Love,
    totally free of worry and care.

I have passed beyond the four qualities.
My heart has torn away the veil of pretense.

There was a time I circled with the nine spheres,
    rolling with the stars across the sky.
There was a time I stayed by his side—
I lived in his world
    and he gave me everything.

With the best of intentions
I became a prisoner in this form.
How else did I get here?
What crime did I commit?
But I'd rather be in a prison with my Friend
    than in a rosegarden all alone.

I came to this world
To have a sight of Joseph's purity.
Like a baby born of its mother's womb,
    I was brought here with blood and tears.

People think they are born only once
But they have been here so many times.

In the cloak of this ragged body
    I have walked countless paths.
How many times I have worn out this cloak!

With ascetics in the desert
    I watched night turn into day.
With pagans in the temple
    I slept at the foot of idols.

I've been a charlatan and a king;
I've been a healer, and fraught with disease.

I've been on my death-bed
    so many times. . . .
Floating up like the clouds
Pouring down like the rain.

As a darvish I sought the dust of annihilation
    but it never touched my robe.
So I gathered armfuls of roses
    in this faded garden of existence.

I am not of wind nor fire
    nor of the stormy seas.
I am not formed out of painted clay.
I am not even Shams-e Tabriz—
    I am the essence of laughter,
    I am pure light.

Look again if you see me—
    It's not me you have seen!

Gone to the Unseen

At last you have departed and gone to the Unseen.
What marvelous route did you take from this world?

Beating your wings and feathers,
    you broke free from this cage.
Rising up to the sky
    you attained the world of the soul.
You were a prized falcon trapped by an Old Woman.
Then you heard the drummer's call
    and flew beyond space and time.

As a lovesick nightingale, you flew among the owls.
Then came the scent of the rosegarden
    and you flew off to meet the Rose.

The wine of this fleeting world
    caused your head to ache.
Finally you joined the tavern of Eternity.
Like an arrow, you sped from the bow
    and went straight for the bull's eye of bliss.

This phantom world gave you false signs
But you turned from the illusion
    and journeyed to the land of truth.

You are now the Sun—
    what need have you for a crown?
You have vanished from this world—
    what need have you to tie your robe?

I've heard that you can barely see your soul.
But why look at all?—
    yours is now the Soul of Souls!

O heart, what a wonderful bird you are.
Seeking divine heights,
Flapping your wings,
    you smashed the pointed spears of your enemy.

The flowers flee from Autumn, but not you—
You are the fearless rose
    that grows amidst the freezing wind.

Pouring down like the rain of heaven
    you fell upon the rooftop of this world.
Then you ran in every direction
    and escaped through the drain spout. . . .

Now the words are over
    and the pain they bring is gone.
Now you have gone to rest
    in the arms of the Beloved.

Part Seven

Stories

The following selections are from Menaqibu el Arifin *(Lives of the Saints), written in the fourteenth century by Ahmed al-Aflaki, a disciple of Rumi's grandson.*

❖

 he wife of Jalal (Rumi), Kira Khatun, called the "Mary of Her Age," had this memory about Shams and her husband:

During the winter, my husband and Shams were in retreat in a room in our house. I was peeking through a crack in the door, trying to see what was happening. All of a sudden the back wall of the room moved apart and six radiant beings entered through the opening. These strangers, who shined with a mystical radiance, greeted Jalal and Shams, and placed a fresh bouquet of flowers in front of them. Then they all sat together, in complete silence, until the hour of the morning worship arrived. Then the men motioned to Shamsuddin to lead the morning service, but he declined. The honor was then given to Jalal who conducted the service with such beauty and humility that it brought tears to my eyes. When the service was over, the six strangers left, passing through the same opening in the wall by which they entered.

Jalal then emerged from the room and came right toward me. He handed me the flowers and said, "Take good care of these."

The next day I took a few flowers from the bouquet to the perfumer's market to find out where these flowers came from, since I had never seen any like them before. Every merchant was astonished by the freshness, the color, and the divine scent of these blossoms. By chance, a spice merchant from India, who was traveling through Konya, saw the flowers and cried out, "These are the petals of a rare flower that only grow in one place in South India. What are they doing here, in Konya, in the middle of the winter?"

I returned home in utter amazement. When I saw Jalal, he urged me to watch over the flowers with great care, as they were a special offering given to me from the gardeners of a secret earthly paradise.

Kira kept the flowers all her life and the petals were used for healing diseases and giving sight to the blind. The flowers were said to be as fragrant and as beautiful as on the day she received them.

◆

A meeting was held at the minister's palace where each guest brought a large candle weighing four or five pounds. Jalal came to the assembly holding a small candle, barely weighing an ounce.

The grandees smiled at this puny candle. Jalal, however, told them that their imposing flames depended on his wick for their light. They all laughed in disbelief. Jalal smiled, looked around, and then blew out his candle—every candle in the hall was extinguished, and the whole company was cast into darkness.

After a few minutes Jalal lit his candle, and once again, all the candles began to burn brightly as before.

One of Jalal's disciples decided to go on a journey to Egypt. His friends tried to dissuade him but without success. The matter was then brought to Jalal who also told him not to take the voyage.

The young man could not shake his desire for adventure, and one night he secretly stole away, heading for Syria. When he arrived in Antioch he joined the crew of a ship and set sail. As fate would have it, his ship was captured by a band of Ferengi pirates. He was taken prisoner, thrown into a dungeon, and given a morsel of food each day, which was just barely enough to keep him alive.

He wept bitterly, and reproached himself for disobeying his master. One night, after forty dreadful days, Jalal came to him in a dream and said: "Tomorrow the misbelievers will come with some questions: always give them the answer 'I know.' By that means you will be released." The next morning, a group of Ferengi people came to the man and said: "Our prince is sick." The disciple answered, "I know." They said, "He might die." The disciple answered, "I know." Then they asked, "Do you know the practice of medicine?" The disciple answered, "I know." So they took him out of the pit, bathed him, dressed him in fine clothes, and led him into the chamber of the infirm prince. The young man, inspired by God, ordered them to bring seven fruits. He added a few herbs, made it into a draught, and urged the ailing prince to drink it.

By the grace of God, and the intercession of the saints, his treatment was crowned with success, and the prince recovered. When the prince was well, he told the young disciple to ask for whatever he might wish. The disciple asked for his freedom so that he might rejoin his master. He then related all that had befallen him—his disobedience, his vision, and the assistance of Jalal. The prince and all his court were so taken by this account that they all became believers in the power of Jalal's grace.

When the disciple arrived home, before going to his own house, he hastened to express his gratitude to Jalal. On seeing his master from afar, he threw himself on the ground, embraced Jalal's feet and wept. Jalal raised him up, kissed both his cheeks, and said: "It was a narrow escape you made. For this you must thank God. From now on remain in this city and make a righteous living. Take contentment as your example. The hardship of the sea, the commotion of the ship, the pain of captivity, and the darkness of a dungeon are full of evils. Be content where you are—contentment is one of God's great blessings."

◆

After Jalal's death, the Mogul general Kigatu Khan and his army approached Konya, intending to destroy the city and massacre its inhabitants.

That night in a dream, Jalal appeared to Kigatu, grabbed him by the throat, and said, "Konya is mine. What do you want from my people?"

The general awoke, fell on his knees, and prayed for mercy. The next day he sent an emissary, asking for permission to enter the city as a guest.

When he arrived at the palace, the dignitaries of the city showered him with rich offerings. The moment he sat down at the court he was seized with a violent tremor, as he saw a man seated on a nearby chair. "Who is that man sitting on the chair next to you?" he

192

asked the prince. The prince looked around but saw no one. "O great Khan," he replied, "no one is sitting by my side." "What are you saying?" asked the general. "By your side I see a tall man with a beard, wearing a gray turban and an Indian plaid over his chest—and he is looking at me most ferociously."

The prince inferred that it was Jalal's spirit, and said, "Only the sacred eyes of majesty are privileged enough to behold such a sight. The one you see is our Lord, Jalaluddin, who is buried in this land."

The Khan replied: "Last night in a dream he al-most choked me to death!—telling me Konya was his possession. Now, Prince, I honor you as I would my own father: I will not touch so much as one stone of your city."

One of Jalal's disciples was a holy woman named Fakhru-n Nisa, "The Glory of Women." She was well known among all the holy men as a woman possessing unsurpassed sanctity. She always attended the meetings at Jalal's house, and he occasionally visited her.

One day her friends suggested that she go on a pilgrimage to Mecca. She agreed but would not begin her journey without first consulting her master. And so she went to see him. As she entered his presence, be-fore she was even able to speak, Jalal called out to her: "O, most wonderful idea! May thy journey bring you the fortune of both worlds! God willing, we shall be there together." She bowed, said nothing, and left the room. All the disciples who saw this were puzzled.

That night she stayed at Jalal's house, praying with him till midnight. At midnight he went up to the terraced roof to perform the divine vigil. When the service was over, he fell into an ecstatic state, shouting and proclaiming the glory of God. Then he called to the room below, where the lady was, and invited her to come up on the roof and join him.

When she arrived, he told her to look upward, saying that her wish was about to be granted. On looking up, she beheld the sacred black stone of Mecca suspended in the air. It was circling Jalal's head, and spinning round like a whirling darvish. It was so plain and distinct as to leave no room for doubt or uncertainty. She fell into a deep trance, which lasted for a short time, but which felt like an eternity. When she came to, she abandoned ideas of making a pilgrimage to Mecca. For she saw that Jalal was her Mecca. What need had she to go anywhere else?

Terms and Symbolism

BELOVED: God and His loving aspects, all of which are accessible to man's immediate experience. One's own soul; the source of one's longing. The lover (soul) searches for the Beloved (God). Can also represent one's Master. Also: Lover, Sweetheart, Friend.

BREEZE: The life-giving breath of the Beloved.

BUBBLE: Individual existence. Man is a bubble compared with the ocean (God). See FOAM.

BURNING: Process of purification of the soul. Longing for God.

CROW: A dark or negative force that often surrounds the soul.

CURLS: See HAIR.

DARVISH: Literally "poor man": one who calls nothing his own. One engaged in spiritual practice under the guidance of a *shaykh* or spiritual Master; a member of a Sufi order. *Dervish* is the Turkish spelling of the Persian word *darvish*. The term "Whirling Dervish" refers to the Sufi order based in Turkey. See MEVLEVI.

DRUNKENNESS: Divine intoxication; a soul's rapture with the love of God.

FACE: God's true form, one not covered by the veils of the world.

FALCON: The soul, often portrayed as trapped in this physical world longing for the wrist of the King (God).

FLUTE: Symbol of longing. The flute, having been cut from the reed bed, spends its life wailing and longing for the day of its return to the source from which it came (the reed bed). In the same way, a Sufi longs to return to the Beloved, the source from which he came. See "Song of the Reed" on page 21.

FOAM: Outward and shallow forms (of limited existence) that cover the depths of the infinite ocean (God).

FRIEND: A term for the Beloved. The Friend symbolizes the Beloved's role as one's most intimate friend; one with whom a seeker can share all his secrets; one who knows the seeker's every thought.

GARDEN: The beauty and bliss of Paradise; a symbol for God's creative power. The place in this world (or the next) where lovers come into the presence of the Beloved. Serenity, beauty, inner peace, and life.

HAIR: The power of illusion, *maya*. Also: tresses, curls, or locks.

IDOL-WORSHIPPER: One who worships idols, as opposed to the one, all-pervasive God. The worship of idols, in the context of Islam (and its Judeo-Christian origins), is seen as sacrilegious, and idol-worshippers are seen as the lowest class of citizens.

IMPOSTER: The aspect of God that tricks the soul into thinking the world is real.

JOSEPH: Joseph is considered the most beautiful person and he represents God's perfect beauty in human form. As told in the Koran, Joseph is taken from his father and placed in the bottom of a well. When a passing caravan dips their bucket into the well for water, they pull up the child Joseph. Joseph is soon sold into slavery. Due to his purity and devotion, Joseph is freed and exalted and eventually reunited with his family. Joseph, in Rumi's work, often represents the soul. His difficult journey outward (away from his father's care) and his triumphant reunion is akin to the soul's journey into the world and its return to the Beloved (its source).

KA'BE: The cube-shaped Muslim shrine at Mecca that encloses the sacred black stone given to Abraham by the angel Gabriel. The Ka'be measures thirty-five feet by forty feet by fifty feet high, and is located in the center of the Great Mosque. It is the holiest of holy places for Muslims, and Muslim worshippers face the Ka'be while praying. Also spelled *Kaaba*. Pronounced <u>cat</u> + <u>bay</u>—ca-BAY.

KHEZR: The prophet or sage who became immortal by drinking from the water of life. Khezr is the patron saint of wandering seekers, appears mysteriously in order to guide them, protect them, and in rare instances, initiate them into the Sufi path. Also spelled *Khidr*.

KILLING: The destruction of one's ego and its limited sense of identity. It refers especially to the breaking of one's attachment to the physical body. The Persian word is *fana*, most commonly translated as "annihilation."

KING: God; a name for the Beloved.

KONYA: A city in present-day Turkey where Rumi lived most of his life, and where his mausoleum is located.

KORAN: The sacred book of the Muslims, containing the revelations of Muhammad.

LANGUAGE OF THE BIRDS: Words of the spirit that transcend the limits of this world.

LAYLA: See MAJNUN.

LOVER: A name for the Beloved. When written with a lowercase *l*, "lover" refers to a Sufi, or a seeker, who longs for the Beloved.

MAJNUN: Majnun represents a lover consumed in the search for his lost beloved. According to the classic story of Layla and Majnun, after gaining one glimpse of Layla, Majnun spends the rest of his days in search of her. As one version of the story goes, when Majnun finally finds her, he has no interest in her because the longing for her became the longing for love itself. Layla's outer form, though beautiful, could not compare with the splendor that Majnun found within himself. Also spelled *Majnoon*.

MAULANA: Literally "Our Master." The name by which Rumi was most commonly addressed by his disciples.

MECCA: The holy city of Islam that is site of the Ka'be; the most important pilgrimage site for Muslims.

MEVLEVI: The Sufi order known in the West as "Whirling Dervishes." This order was inspired by Rumi, and its name comes from the Turkish pronunciation of *Maulana* ("Our Master"), a title given to Rumi.

NIGHTINGALE: A soul that longs for the Beloved or its quality of eternal beauty (represented by the rose).

OCEAN: God. The universe. That which is limitless.

PARTY: A Sufi gathering, characterized by ecstatic dancing and revelry in God's love. Also: celebration.

PEARL: The perfection and beauty of one's true self. Divine wisdom.

PRAYER ROCK: A small rock used by Muslims during prayers to mark the position where the head must touch in order to face the Ka'be in Mecca.

PROPHET, THE: Muhammad; founder of the Muslim faith.

REBEC: Persian instrument played with a bow.

ROSE: The eternal and perfect beauty of the Beloved.

ROSEGARDEN: Paradise and its eternal beauty. See GARDEN.

RUBAAB: A stringed instrument often played with a bow. Pronounced like "rhubarb" without the second r— RU-bahb.

RUBA'I: From the Arabic meaning "foursome," a four-line poem (quatrain) of Persian origin, with the first, second, and fourth lines rhyming. Plural: *rubá'iyát*.

SAAQI: Cupbearer. Barmaid; woman in a tavern who goes from table to table pouring wine. She represents divine grace and a form of the Beloved who intoxicates the soul by pouring the wine of love. The image comes from the Koran, which describes God as "He who gives to drink." Pronounced sod + ghee—sa-GHEE.

SA'MAA: Literally "audition." The sacred whirling dance of the darvishes, in which the motions of the human body represent the movements of the universe. The term also refers to any Sufi practice that involves music and chanting. Pronounced <u>semi</u> + <u>ah</u>—sem-AH; or <u>some</u> + <u>ah</u>—sum-AH. Also spelled *sema, sama*.

SHAMS-E TABRIZ: "The Glorious Sun of Tabriz." Rumi's spiritual master, who came from Tabriz, an ancient city in northwest Iran. Also called *Shamsuddin, Shams Din, Shams*.

SHAYKH: A spiritual master of the Islamic tradition.

SHIRT (TORN OPEN): The torn shirt or the tearing of one's shirt is an expression of grief and despair, the exposing of one's heart to the torments of the Beloved.

SUFI: From the Arabic root *suf*, "wool," referring to the wool garments worn by the earliest Sufis; but also from *safa*, "purity." A Sufi is a member of the mystical order of Islam based on love and devotion.

SULTAN WALAD: Rumi's eldest son, who formally established the Mevlevi order of Whirling Dervishes.

SWEETHEART: An endearing name for the Beloved.

TAVERN: A place where Sufis gather to dance and drink the "wine" of God's love.

TWO WORLDS: Heaven and earth. This world and the next.

WATER OF LIFE: The nectar of immortality; the life-giving water of God; the primordial waters of creation.

WE: A reference to God. In Islamic literature, God often speaks to devotees with the term "We" as opposed to

"I," God being the whole of human existence and, in that form, plural. Also: Us.

WEDDING NIGHT: The night the soul (the lover) joins in union with God (the Beloved). It also refers to the day a great saint leaves this world.

WINE: Nectar; the intoxicating love of God.

Sources

Primary Sources:

Aflaki, Shems al Din Ahmad, James Redhouse, trans. *Menaaquibu al Arifin* (*Legends of the Sufis*) (Wheaton, Illinois: The Theosophical Publishing House, 1976).

Arberry, A. J., trans. *Mystical Poems of Rumi* (Chicago: University of Chicago Press, 1968).

———, trans. *Mystical Poems of Rumi 2* (Chicago: University of Chicago Press, 1991).

Chittick, William. *The Sufi Path of Love* (Albany: SUNY Press, 1983).

Furuzanfar, Badi-uz Zaman. *Kulliyat-e Shams* (Tehran: Amir Kabir Press, 1957–66; Tehran: University of Tehran, 1963), Vol. 8.

Nicholson, R. A. trans. *Rumi: Divani Shams Tabriz* (San Francisco: The Rainbow Bridge, 1973).

Shiva, Shahram. *Rending the Veil* (Prescott, Arizona: Hohm Press, 1995).

Vitray-Meyerovitch, Eva de. *Odes Mystiques* (Paris: Editions Klincksiek, 1984).

Sources Consulted:

Baldick, Julian. *Mystical Islam: An Introduction to Sufism* (New York: New York University Press, 1980).

Ergin, Nevit O., trans. *Divan-i Kebir* (Sun Valley, California: Echo Publications, 1995).

Goldin, Marylin. "Love Is the Flame Which Burns Everything." *Darshan Magazine,* vol. 14, pp. 71–84; and vol. 15, pp 79–85.

Helminski, Edmund. *The Ruins of the Heart* (Putney, Vermont: Threshold Books, 1981).

Iqbal, Afzal. *The Life and Work of Jalaluddin Rumi* (London: Octagon Press, 1983).

Khosla, K. *The Sufism of Rumi* (Longmead, UK: Element Books Ltd, 1987).

Moyne, John, and Coleman Barks. *Open Secret* (Putney, Vermont: Threshold Books, 1984).

———. *Unseen Rain: Quatrains of Rumi* (Putney, Vermont: Threshold Books, 1986).

Nicholson, R. A. *The Mystics of Islam* (New York: Shocken Books, 1975).

Schimmel, Annemarie. *I Am Wind, You Are Fire* (Boston: Shambhala Publications, 1992).

———. *Look! This Is Love* (Boston: Shambhala Publications, 1991).

———. *Mystical Dimensions of Islam* (Chapel Hill: University of North Carolina Press, 1975).

———. *The Triumphal Sun* (London: East-West Publications, 1978).

Vitray-Meyerovitch, Eva de, Simone Fattal, trans. *Rumi and Sufism* (Sausalito, California: The Post-Apollo Press, 1987).

Williams, John A. *Islam* (New York: George Braziller, 1962).

Wilson, Peter L., and Nasrollah Pourjavady. *The Drunken Universe* (Grand Rapids, Michigan: Phanes Press, 1987).

Index

The numerals in brackets refer to the number assignments found in various editions of Rumi's poetry: numerals alone refer to poems found in Kulliyat-e Shams, edited by Badi-uz Zaman Furuzanfar, published by Amir Kabir Press; numerals preceded by "N" refer to poems found in R. A. Nicholson's Rumi: Divani Shams Tabriz; numerals preceded by "E" refer to poems found in Nevit O. Ergin, Divan-i Kebir, volume 2. (See "Sources" for complete citations of these works.)

All quatrains are based on literal translations by Shahram Shiva, most of which can be found in Rending the Veil.

Odes

"All My Youth Returns" [207], 16
"Ashes of Union, The" [3071], 174
"Ball of Wax, A" [1374], 160
"Better than Cabbage Soup" [1739], 154
"Birds of Paradise, The" [1713], 65
"Black Cloud, The" [636], 150
"Blast of That Trumpet, The" [1145], 171
"Bread of Egypt, The" [981], 137
"Breath of My Presence, The" [1945], 35
"By the Curl of My Hair" [2509], 9
"Dome of the Inner Sky, The" [1426], 123
"Don't Go Without Me" [2195], 6
"Don't Sleep" [312], 84
"From Black Soot" [2290], 31
"From self to Self" [1142], 70
"Glitter of This Fantasy, The" [463], 130
"Gone to the Unseen" [3051], 184
"He Also Made the Key" [2820], 28
"He Gives to Taste" [765], 94
"I Am a Painter" [1462], 153

"I Cried Out at Midnight" [1335], 102
"In Silence" [1897], 162
"Inner Sunrise" [2996], 120
"Lies!" [1299], 146
"Like This" [1826], 79
"Love Tricks" [566], 112
"Lover Without a Tear, A" [721], 138
"Master San'ai" [996], 178
"Mine of Rubies, A" [2015], 119
"My King" [1393], 107
"No Place to Hide" [2251], 140
"O Beloved, Be Like That to Me" [E117], 26
"On the First Day" [N17], 18
"On the Threshold" [1789], 61
"One Lasting Truth" [861], 40
"Only Through This" [3090], 148
"Prince of Eternity" [1317], 142
"Pure Light" [N332], 182
"Return, The" [1353], 12
"Roses Are in Bloom!, The" [330], 54
"Sacred Blasphemy, A" [1869], 90
"Shepherd's Care, The" [2577], 58
"Soft Petals" [2389], 74
"Song of the Reed" [from the *Masnavi*], 21
"Song to My Soul" [1725], 14
"This Eternal Play" [649], 126
"Thousand Souls of Mine, A" [3050], 10
"Through an Open Window" [1888], 158
"Throw Down Your Staff" [123], 134
"We Can See the Truth in Your Eyes" [120], 3
"When All You Had Was Him" [N32], 48
"Who Is at My Door?" [436], 98
"Willing Slaves" [1077], 128
"Wood for His Fire" [3061], 44
"Your Golden Cup" [310], 36
"Your Triumphant Song" [911], 167

Quatrains

A poet I am not [1256], 136
All night I danced round the house of my Beloved [171], 42
Alone, like the Sun in the sky—come back [64], 22

Blood from the heart of lovers [656], 111
Don't ask me about prayer rocks— [62], 78
Don't be like a sparrow [46], 144
Don't come to our party without a drum! [1322], 53
Don't talk about night anymore!— [232], 82
Don't turn from the delight [1575], 64
Every day my heart cries out [925], 92
Every question I ask is about you [1194], 30
He said, I'll turn you round like a treadmill [348], 106
Hold to the reins of Love and don't be afraid [985], 157
I dreamt that the Beloved entered my body [167], 105
I knocked on the door [711], 46
I said [1889], 101
I said, This longing in my heart [1234], 175
I want nothing to do with this world or the next [366], 72
I'm in a daze [15], 47
In the heavens I see your eyes [1127], 8
In the lover's heart is a lute [465], 69
In their seeking [306], 177
In this world of love [1365], 180
I've been dead to this world for a long time [52], 34
Last night you fell asleep on me! [1683], 20
Like a flower's sweet nectar [1695], 127
My crippled poetry began to dance [906], 38
My face is yellow with regret—don't ask me why [986], 97
O eyes, rub your shirt in blood [1015], 83
O flute [79], 104
O heart [1012], 76
O precious soul [1449t], 115
O seeker [1923], 89
O soul [1915], 156
O tulip, come and learn [942], 77
O weary heart [840], 43
Our garden is filled with nightingales [1050], 68
See that caravan of camels [34], 39
Soul of all souls, life of all life—you are That [419], 5
The day your love touches me [720], 27
The face of your religion [1825], 145
The living world of pure Consciousness—you are That [1921], 181
The mountain of your imagination [704], 93
The secret Heart-Ravisher has been exposed! [996], 100
The secrets of eternity are beyond us [7], 169
The seeds of His love blossom in every heart [681b], 56

There is a place where words are born of silence [465], 25
Walk by my grave and you'll become drunk [791], 60
We drink the wine of our own blood [1306], 57
We're not ahead, we're behind [1311], 73
When I shed tears of blood [527], 114
When we were bound, He added another chain [809], 95
When you move around Saturn, you become the heavens [1709], 121
Who said the eternal one has died? [806], 152
With every breath I plant the seeds of devotion— [1183], 170
You have made me weary [1277], 110
You have two hands, two legs, and two eyes [18], 33
You searched the whole world for life [1601], 133
Your heart is the size of an ocean— [31], 132
You've been here only a few days [405], 139

About the Author

Jonathan Star graduated with honors from Harvard University, where he studied Eastern religion and architecture. For the past fifteen years he has pursued spiritual practice, both Zen Meditation and Yogic disciplines.

Mr. Star's poetry and writings have been translated into several languages. His works include *Two Suns Rising, A Garden Beyond Paradise,* and a translation of the *Tao Te Ching.*